Landing on Your North Star

A guide to finding your life's purpose

Peggi Cooney, MSW
and
Brigitta Dau, Certified Life Coach

Leaning Rock Press
Gales Ferry, CT 06335

Leaning Rock Press
Gales Ferry, CT 06335
leaningrockpress@gmail.com
www.leaningrockpress.com

978-1-960596-83-3, Softcover

Publisher's Cataloging-In-Publication Data
(Prepared by Cassidy Cataloguing's PCIP Service)

Names:	Cooney, Peggi, author. | Dau, Brigitta, author.
Title:	Landing on your North Star : a guide to finding your life's purpose / Peggi Cooney and Brigitta Dau.
Description:	Gales Ferry, CT : Leaning Rock Press, [2026] | Includes bibliographical references and index.
Identifiers:	ISBN: 9781960596833 (softcover)
Subjects:	LCSH: Self-actualization (Psychology) | Self-realization. | Change (Psychology) | Diaries--Authorship. | Meditation. | LCGFT: Self-help publications. | BISAC: SELF-HELP / Personal Growth / General. | SELF-HELP / Journaling. | SELF-HELP / Meditations.
Classification:	LCC: BF637.S4 C66 2026 | DDC: 158.1--dc23

Dedicated to...

The dreamers, the seekers, and the doers -

to everyone daring to live fully, love deeply, and

forge the extraordinary life that is already within you.

PRAISE FOR *Landing on Your North Star*

In *Landing on Your North Star* you have a playful and entirely effective way to create your life on purpose and in alignment with who you are at your core. With all the static in the world right now, the best you can do is go within and attune to the guidance of your heart. When you claim and get to know your North Star, life lines up accordingly. This book is a delightful companion on one of the most meaningful journeys you will ever take, the one home to yourself.

– Whitney Freya, Inspired Living Expert WhitneyFreya.com

"*Landing on Your North Star* is a powerful reminder that clarity doesn't come from doing more, but from getting rooted in what truly matters. Peggi and Brigitta partnered seamlessly to create a guide that inspires readers to reach for their goals no matter the challenge in front of them. In a noisy, often divisive world, this book cuts through the clutter. It clears the mind, grounds the reader in intention, core values, and meaningful goals, and guides execution in a way that feels calm, purposeful, and true to oneself. This is not a pressure-filled roadmap. It's an invitation to lead your life with alignment, courage, and self-trust.

– Toni Will, Author of Rebellious Success & General Manager, Kalamazoo Wings (ECHL)

Table of Contents

Peggi Cooney and Brigitta Dau

Forward/Introductions

Why Landing on Your North Star Matters

"Do the best you can until you know better. Then when you know better, do better."
-Maya Angelou

Finding your North Star, your guiding purpose or core values, is important because it serves as a steady reference point in both your personal and professional life. Your North Star helps you define what truly matters to you. It acts like a compass, guiding your decisions, goals, and actions. When you're faced with uncertainty or choices, your North Star helps you stay aligned with your deeper values.

When things get tough, as they do because we are human, having a clear purpose helps you stay grounded. It reminds you of why you started what you're working toward, making it easier to persevere during those challenging times that are sure to come.

A North Star fosters consistency in your behavior and decisions. It helps you act in alignment with your values, which builds trust with others and strengthens your own sense of integrity. Purpose-driven people often feel more energized and fulfilled. Your North Star connects your daily tasks to a bigger picture, making even mundane work feel meaningful.

With a clear guiding principle, you can evaluate opportunities and challenges more effectively. You're less likely to be swayed by short-term gains or external pressures that don't align with your long-term vision.

We have borrowed North Star strategies from many sources to bring a comprehensive interactive book to help you answer questions like:

- What kind of values do I hold most dearly?
- What kind of impact do I want to have on the world?
- What makes me feel most alive or fulfilled?

Introductions

"Don't ask what the world needs. Ask what makes you come alive, and go do it."
-Howard Thurman

We, the Gnomes of the North Star, Gnorth and Gnora, are grateful and excited to have you here. Think of us as your personal assistants from the future. We are here to help you achieve your desires and live your life in alignment with your own personal "North Star". We will be with you as you plot your path, celebrate your wins, achieve your goals and bring your dreams to life. We are here to guide you when you're feeling apprehensive, offer a little light when you are in darkness, and provide gentle advice when you are feeling overwhelmed.

We tasked two of our favorite humans with the job of creating this workbook. Think of this book as your master guide for brainstorming, dream catching, and goal mapping. Use it as your soul's compass to help you chart your journey towards your North Star.

Meet our facilitators

Brigitta:

I've always loved journaling and personal growth, long before becoming a Life Coach and Reiki Master. I also know that our happiness is not based on one aspect of our lives. We are complex people with many layers of experience. For years, I searched for a book that would allow me to explore all those facets through one inclusive lens. When I couldn't find it, I began writing the book I wished existed. That was years ago. When I decided to give up alcohol in 2022, I had the privilege of meeting Peggi. I was already a fan of her book, *This Side of Alcohol*, and jumped at the chance to connect with her through her virtual book club. In one of her talks, she spoke about finding your "North Star". Her description perfectly matched the book I'd been yearning for. I knew I had to reach out and convince her that together, we could combine our resources to create something fun, practical, and empowering.

And, shhhhhhh… Gnorth and Gnora are totally unaware that I created them and that they aren't actually real. Full disclosure, I'm a bit of a compulsive gnome knitter. Since gnomes are often seen as guardians of hidden treasures and keepers of wisdom with a little whimsical thrown in, I thought they would make perfect guides for Landing on Your North Star.

Peggi:

When Brigitta proposed writing this book with her, I jumped at the opportunity. I love sharing the things I have learned as a social worker, sobriety advocate, and as an intrepid woman who has lived on this planet for over seven decades. Although this is not a book about recovery, it is a book about setting and reaching goals, and on a bigger scale, finding your life's purpose. It has been so much fun for me to share tools that can help us discover and stay focused on our North Star. As one of my favorite poets, Mary Oliver, puts it best:

> "Tell me, what else should I have done? Doesn't everything die at last and too soon?
> Tell me, what is it you plan to do with your one wild and precious life?" [1]

Peggi Cooney and Brigitta Dau

Book Basics

"There will never be a right time. Stop waiting and start doing."
-Mel Robbins

We created this book to be your own personal map to discovering and staying in alignment with your North Star, with comprehensive and interactive strategies for guidance. Our hope is that by the end of this book, you will have a clear vision forward to creating a life you are passionate about. Read this book at a pace that works for you. Take your time with it, reading one chapter a week, or devouring the whole thing in one weekend. You could even do this with friends as a stay-at-home or destination empowerment retreat.

Both of us use the activities in this book consistently in our own lives and with the clients we serve. You may find yourself using this book repeatedly as a "go-to" goal-setting resource.

Gnorth recommends, Have FUN with the activities! Creating goals with soul should be done with verve and enthusiasm.

Each chapter begins with a mindfulness visualization. We recommend not skipping the meditation exercises. Meditation is profoundly important in the journey to find your North Star, your deepest purpose or guiding truth, because it creates the inner conditions necessary for clarity, alignment, and insight. We both consider meditation practice as mini spas that promote personal grounding and wellness.

Here's how it connects:

- **Quiets the noise:** We live in a world full of distractions, expectations, and external influences. Meditation helps silence mental chatter, create space for inner wisdom to emerge, and reduce the influence of fear, ego, and comparison. Your North Star isn't found in the noise—it's discovered in stillness.

- **Deepens self-awareness:** Meditation is a practice of turning inward. It allows you to observe your thoughts and emotions without judgment, recognize patterns and beliefs that may be blocking your path, and connect you with your authentic self, beyond roles and labels.
- **Strengthens intuition**: Your North Star often speaks in whispers, not shouts. Meditation sharpens your ability to listen to subtle inner signals, builds trust in your own inner guidance, and helps you distinguish between intuition and impulse.
- **Cultivates presence:** The journey to your North Star isn't just about the destination—it's about being fully present along the way. Meditation teaches mindfulness, which keeps you in the now; acceptance, which helps you embrace the journey; and patience, which allows your purpose to unfold naturally.
- **Opens insight and creativity**: In meditation, the mind becomes a fertile ground for breakthrough ideas, creative visions, and unexpected clarity.

Following the meditation are topics, strategies and real-life examples that reflect the our diverse experiences, personally and professionally. Everyone has a unique background, personality, and way of processing the world. By offering a charcuterie of practices, you can find the ones that truly speak to you.

In a world overflowing with advice on how to live with purpose, it's easy to feel overwhelmed—or worse, like you're doing it wrong. The truth is, there is no single, universal method for discovering your North Star. The guiding light—your deepest sense of direction, meaning, and clarity—looks different for everyone. And the journey to find it? Just as unique. That's why this book offers a variety of strategies to help you uncover your North Star. Whether you're someone who thrives on reflection, action, creativity, or connections, there's a path here for you. Some of you may find your truth through journaling or meditation. Some of you may need to walk through nature, engage in deep conversation, or revisit childhood dreams. There's no wrong way—only your way.

Including multiple approaches isn't just about choice. It's about respecting the diversity of the human experience. It's about acknowledging that what works for one person may not work for another—and that's okay. In fact, it's beautiful. The richness of our lives comes from the many ways we seek and find meaning.

At the end of every chapter, there are activities that will assist you in discovery, goal setting, and staying the course. Ultimately, this book is designed to support you with clarification, planning, and overcoming potential obstacles. After reading each chapter, we encourage you to do all of the activities as that is where the greatest personal growth happens.

And we suggest you treat yourself to a dedicated journal for all the activities. Journals can be as inexpensive as the ones that can be found for seven dollars at TJ Max, or choose one that floats your boat at places like Barnes and Noble. Find your perfect pen and/or markers. Make it yours. Returning to your journal can be a very cathartic and insightful experience. Peggi's journal turned into a published book. Excerpts of Brigitta's journal have become topics for her workshops.

So as you move through this book, think of it as a toolbox. Try different tools. Mix and match. Return to the ones that resonate. Leave behind what doesn't. Your North Star isn't a destination—it's a relationship. And like any meaningful relationship, it deserves time, attention, and a willingness to explore. After all, this is your life, and you are embarking on a journey to discover what really matters to YOU. So, grab your journal and cozy up with this book. Take all the time you need to discover your North Star.

Gnora reminds us: You may miss out on valuable insights by rushing or skipping sections.

Setting the Mood:

We Are All Magnificent Creatives

"Creativity is intelligence having fun."
-Albert Einstein

Gnorth reminds us of this fact: We colored before we wrote and sang before we spoke.

We are creative by nature. Our very evolution is based on "creative thinking". Having fun is an important aspect of living a purposeful life.

And let's be honest. Taking risks, creating new realities, and busting through our internal obstacles is often hard work. The bigger the goal, the bigger the challenge. Hopefully, the bigger the payoff. But, as we point out in this book, setting a big goal is less about actually achieving the goal; it's more about who we become as we journey towards it. Our goals should stretch us to reach outside of our comfort zone.

As human beings, we naturally go to the place of least resistance, traveling the same road over and over. However, do you ever notice that by doing so, we just create ruts? Quoting Einstein: "Insanity is doing the same thing over and over again and expecting a different result." To engage in deep learning, one has to develop new neural pathways.

People learn better when they are challenging themselves just outside their ability—where things are not too hard and not too easy. In this state of deep learning when we are trying to accomplish something difficult, we lay thicker neural networks, meaning that our new skill becomes more potent.

Gnora's observation: Growth and comfort rarely co-exist.

We do this by creating opportunities to celebrate and play along the way. Embracing and expressing our creative side is the fastest way to bring fun into our days. Its also a highly effective tool for tapping into our problem-solving skills. But first, let's talk about how we can express our creativity.

We recommend scheduling times to participate in any form of creative play. Julia Cameron assigns "Artist Dates" as weekly homework assignments in her book, *The Artist's Way*. She explains, "An artist date is a block of time, perhaps two hours weekly, especially set aside and committed to nurturing your creative consciousness, your inner artist."[2]

Once a week might feel overwhelming, but once a month is doable for all of us. So, scheduling and committing to this might mean signing up for a watercolor class or planning a trip to your local art supply shop. Adult coloring books (there are so many really cool ones out there), pens, and pencils and crayons are available at every drugstore in the nation, so there is no excuse not to find some way to play at least once a month.

Stickers are a great way to show your creative side. They are readily available (again, at every drugstore, Michaels, Amazon, or Target) and you can choose a sticker for each day's journal entry. Brigitta uses stickers all over her day planner: "It's true! No matter how busy I am, I certainly have time to peel off a sticker and give myself a gold star for a job well done!" Peggi uses stickers to decorate her day planner and her journals. "They are visual reminders of what I was doing during that time period."

Our friend Stacy, the talented artist behind this book's cover, used bee stickers to mark each day she didn't use THC. She recently got a beautiful bee tattoo to remind her of her new lifestyle choice.

If you're interested in doing a little more than sticker art, consider "junk journaling". This is literally cutting and pasting. Start with the journal you are using alongside this book. Instead of writing, record your thoughts and feelings with images. If you are feeling ambitious, you could paint or draw your ideas. But if you are feeling intimidated by that (we can relate!), flip through a magazine and cut out some images that express your feelings. Paste them into your journal. Add to this journal page as you find images and enjoy how your artwork gradually comes to life.

You lose the valuable "hands-on" benefits of creative expression when clicking and dragging a picture on your iPad or laptop, versus actually cutting it out and pasting it on something tangible. The act of choosing pictures and images, cutting them out, deciding their positioning, and pasting them on paper requires us to utilize both sides of our brains. According to Rita Carter, author of *Mapping the Mind*, "the communication between the two lobes of the brain is the goal of creative drive. The thicker the corpus callosum--the aspect responsible for this communication--the more efficiently the brain synchronizes its activities. This, in turn, suppresses the "critical thinking" aspect of our prefrontal cortex which allows for more novel connections and new ideas."[3]

In other words, getting busy with your hands creates more opportunities for growth and learning than clicking a keyboard or tapping a screen. Take the time to cut and paste. Let your fingers get sticky and make a bit of a mess. It's worth the time and effort, and your spirit will thank you for it.

Travel journals are also a lovely way to document your feelings and experiences on your trips. By cutting and pasting images, mementos, brochures, etc. you can recreate the memories of your travels in a creative, playful way. Travel itself is another way to fine-tune your North Star goals because it widens your experiences and expands your choices. If you are feeling more adventurous, try something entirely new. Take a class, read a book, or find some sort of instruction. There are lots of YouTube videos, educational websites and in-person classes available.

Gnorth adds: If you decide to go to an in-person class, you'll also benefit from the community connection you'll find there.

How do you find a local crafting class? Google local studios, and local arts supply stores. They often offer an array of adult crafting classes and have all the supplies necessary to get started. Also, check out apps like "MeetUp", and "Nextdoor" for local groups of like-minded people.

How do you choose which craft to try? Think back to your childhood and notice what you enjoyed doing. We were all creative when we were kids. Did you like coloring? Painting? Making music? Playing in the dirt? See what sparks the inner child in you. What sounds like FUN? And then, go try it.

What has this got to do with landing on your North Star? As mentioned earlier, engaging our creativity enhances our "problem solving" skills.

From Arzu Tahsin & Rosemary Davidson, authors of Craftfulness:

> When we are absorbed in the process of making, our minds can rest and roam. Feelings and ideas that might otherwise be blocked or drowned out by demands of directed thinking, take root and hopefully inspire new ideas, projects, and creations…
>
> …Research also indicates that a number of activities where the brain and the hand connect in absorbing and deliberate repetitive focused movements, (such as knitting, weaving, sewing, chopping vegetables) can be useful for diffusing stress and freeing the mind from unhelpful rumination and negative thinking loops.[4]

We've all had direct experience of this. Think back to a time when you couldn't think of someone's name. Likely you thought, "I'll do something else, and it will pop into my head." And it DID pop into your head, didn't it? That was not some funky trick. That's exactly how our brains work when we allow them to look for solutions in a more creative way.

Activity 1: Schedule Time to Play at Least Once a Month

Getting messy with watercolors or crayons may help you demolish your "writer's block". Cutting and pasting pretty pictures may reveal solutions to your obstacles as you tackle your North Star goals.

Your morning routine (see Chapter Eleven), is a lovely place to incorporate creativity. By doing this, you can guarantee you'll be bringing a little play into your life each day.

PART ONE

YOUR NORTH STAR DEFINED

In a world that often pulls us in a thousand directions, clarity is not a luxury—it's a necessity. *Landing on Your North Star* is about reclaiming that clarity by discovering the inner compass that guides you to your most authentic life. It's not about perfection or having all the answers. It's about alignment (a word you will see so many times throughout the book). It's living in a way that reflects who you truly are and what you deeply value.

We begin our journey with three essential elements:

- Settling on Your Core Values
- South Stars
- Landing on Your North Star

Remember, this book is an invitation to pause, reflect, and realign. Whether you're navigating a transition, seeking deeper meaning, or simply feeling called to live more authentically, your North Star is waiting to be discovered. And once you find it, everything begins to make sense—not because life gets easier, but because you know where you're going.

Peggi Cooney and Brigitta Dau

Chapter One

Your Core Values

"Whatever things you go through, you stay true to who you are and your core values."
–Sophie Gregoire Trudeau

Meditation: 5,4,3,2,1 Breathing

Close your eyes and take a long, deep breath.

For the next **five** inhales and exhales, notice FIVE things that you can hear. You may spend more than a breath on each sound. Simply listen, notice, and breathe while noting what you are hearing in this present moment.

For the next **four** inhales, notice what you can smell. What are FOUR different smells that you can notice in this present moment?

Open your eyes. For the next **three** inhales and exhales, notice THREE things that you can see. You may spend more than a breath on each item. Simply breathe and notice what you are seeing in this present moment.

Now repeat this for the count of **two**, this time noticing what you are touching. Are you sitting on a chair or a couch? Are your feet on the floor? Are you in shoes? Socks? Barefoot?

For **one** breath, notice if you have a taste in your mouth. Just notice.

You can do this meditation as outlined or choose to focus on just a single "sense" for 3 minutes.

Settling on Your Core Beliefs/Values

Core values define what truly matters to you, not what others think should matter to you. If your North Star is not aligned with your values—the things you deeply care about—you risk chasing goals that feel hollow or unsatisfying.

Knowing your core values before landing on your North Star is essential because your values act as the foundation for everything else. Understanding your core beliefs/values can significantly help in discovering your purpose by providing a framework for decision-making and guiding you towards actions that align with your deepest beliefs and aspirations. Core values act as a compass, clarifying what truly matters to you by shaping your priorities, which in turn helps you identify meaningful goals and a sense of direction in life.

Your core values act as a roadmap for discovering your purpose in the following areas:

- Clarity and Direction
- Alignment and Authenticity
- Goal Setting and Prioritization
- Navigating Challenges and Dilemmas
- Understanding our Strengths and Passions,
- Increased Self-Awareness and Confidence

By understanding your values, you gain clarity, direction, and a sense of authenticity, which are essential ingredients for living a life that is both meaningful and fulfilling.

Activity 1: Choosing Your Core Beliefs

"Your values are quiet but persistent navigational tools. When you align your daily behavior with what matters most, you begin to shape a life where what you love, what you're good at, what you're called to do, and how you serve others naturally converge. That's where purpose lives and where leadership begins."
- Angie Chaplin, The Way Onward

Instructions:

1. To determine your core beliefs, use the cards beginning on page 21. All of the cards are listed for reference on page 20. We reccomend cutting out the cards on pages 21, 23, 25, 27 and 29. You can leave them in a pile or spread them out on the floor. Simply read through them and put them in a "Feels Like me" pile, "Might sound like me" pile or a "Not like me" pile.

Gnorth adds: Don't overthink this, friends! Your gut knows what resonates. Trust those first instincts—they're usually spot-on. If you're second-guessing every card, you're probably in your head instead of your heart.

2. Narrow the piles by going back through the "Feels like me" and "Might sound like me" piles. This time, think a little more carefully as you go through them. Be extremely aware of the cards you feel like you should choose (external pressures such as church, ethnicity, culture or family.)

3. Combine the two piles to form one single pile. Go through them again and put the core beliefs that seem to go together in a stack. For example, Wellness and Wellbeing might be grouped together. Integrity, Honesty, and Accountability might go together. Create a maximum of five groupings. If you have more than five, drop the ones least important to you.

4. Finally, choose a single word from each of the five groups that you feel best embodies all the words from that whole group. Again, do not overthink your single word choice. There isn't a right or wrong answer. Go with your gut. Let your subconscious lead the way by picking those cards that feel right to you.

5. Those five cards are your CORE BELIEFS. They are the building blocks for landing on your North Star.

(Adapted with permission from The Way Onward by Angie Chaplin)[5]

FEELS LIKE ME	MIGHT SOUND LIKE ME
NOT LIKE ME	ABUNDANCE
ACCOUNTABILITY	ACHIEVEMENT
BELONGING	CHALLENGE
CLARITY	COLLABORATION
COMMITMENT	COMMUNICATION

COMPASSION	COMMUNITY
CONNECTION	COURAGE
CREATIVITY	CURIOSITY
DEPENDABILITY	DISCIPLINE
DIVERSITY	EMPATHY
EQUALITY	EQUITY

EXCELLENCE	FAITH
FAMILY	FLEXIBILITY
FREEDOM	GRACE
GENEROSITY	GRATITUDE
GROWTH	HAPPINESS
HEALTH	HONESTY

HOPE	HUMOR
INCLUSION	INTEGRITY
INTELLIGENCE	JOY
KINDNESS	LEARNING
LOVE	LOYALTY
PEACE	PURPOSE

RESILIENCE	SECURITY
SERVICE	STRENGTH
SUCCESS	SPIRITUALITY
VULNERABILITY	WELLBEING
WELLNESS	WISDOM

FEELS LIKE ME	MIGHT SOUND LIKE ME
NOT LIKE ME	ABUNDANCE
ACCOUNTABILITY	ACHIEVEMENT
BELONGING	CHALLENGE
CLARITY	COLLABORATION
COMMITMENT	COMMUNICATION

COMPASSION	COMMUNITY
CONNECTION	COURAGE
CREATIVITY	CURIOSITY
DEPENDABILITY	DISCIPLINE
DIVERSITY	EMPATHY
EQUALITY	EQUITY

EXCELLENCE	FAITH
FAMILY	FLEXIBILITY
FREEDOM	GRACE
GENEROSITY	GRATITUDE
GROWTH	HAPPINESS
HEALTH	HONESTY

HOPE	HUMOR
INCLUSION	INTEGRITY
INTELLIGENCE	JOY
KINDNESS	LEARNING
LOVE	LOYALTY
PEACE	PURPOSE

RESILIENCE	SECURITY
SERVICE	STRENGTH
SUCCESS	SPIRITUALITY
VULNERABILITY	WELLBEING
WELLNESS	WISDOM

Peggi's Core Values: Love, Connection, Curiosity, Integrity, Humor

Brigitta's Core Values: Creativity, Connection, Service, Growth, Humor

Peggi Cooney and Brigitta Dau

Chapter Two

South Stars

"The Most impactful things you do are often the things you don't do."
-Mark Manson

Meditation: Center and Gather

Take a deep breath. Either sitting or standing, plant your feet firmly on the ground. Take several deep breaths, paying full attention to your inhales and exhales.

Imagine your spine as a column of light. Imagine this light pulsing outward with every inhale. Feel how you can emanate energy from within your spinal column. You could imagine this as your central column of light.

Reach your arms out wide and imagine you are inviting back any lost or fragmented energy that you may have accidentally leaked at some point. Without judgement as to why or how it escaped, call back your energy now. Ask for it to be returned to you in the best condition possible…a vibrational match to your highest good.

Silently state, or say out loud:
"I call back any of my energy that might have escaped, or been leaked, or lost. I ask that this energy return to me fully healed and perfectly calibrated to support my highest good."

Feel this energy return to your central column of light.

South Stars: Are You on the Right Path?

Have you thought your life might be on the wrong path? We can first find out a lot about our North Star by determining what it isn't. Have you ever observed a behavior in another person and declared to yourself, "I don't want to be that kind of person," or "I am not going to be that kind of leader."

Recognizing what kind of person you don't want to be can save you from burnout, misalignment, or regret. Consider the following:

- Do you feel constantly drained or unfulfilled? Even if you are achieving milestones, you feel emotionally or spiritually empty. Success feels hollow.
- Are you acting in a way that conflicts with your core values? Are you succeeding externally but losing yourself internally?
- Do you keep asking, "Is this all there is?"

In her essay "*Not This*", Elizabeth Gilbert nails this concept:

> Most of us, at some point in our lives (unless we have done everything perfectly… which is: nobody) will have to face a terrible moment in which we realize that we have somehow ended up in the wrong place — or at least, in a very bad place.
>
> Maybe we will have to admit that we are in the wrong job. Or the wrong relationship. With the wrong people around us. Living in the wrong neighborhood. Acting out on the wrong behaviors. Using the wrong substances. Pretending to believe things that we no longer believe. Pretending to be something we were never meant to be.
>
> This moment of realization is seldom fun. In fact, it's terrifying.
>
> We call this moment of realization: "NOT THIS."[6]

A word from Gnora: Sometimes the universe shows us exactly what we DON'T want so we'll finally pay attention to what we DO want. Those 'yuck' moments? They're actually gifts pointing you toward your 'YES!

"Not This" can also be referred to as a "South Star." Experiencing South Stars can be so helpful in directing us to our North Stars. Rob Bell, author, podcaster, and former pastor believes that we can be inspired by someone else's North Star when it resonates with you and what you want to be or do. Other people's North Stars show us something about ourselves. And yet, Bell believes that South Stars can be even more powerful than North ones in finding our true purpose.

Bell's invitation to you "is to begin to find inspiration and energy and guidance in all the South Stars around you. There's all kinds of North Stars around us, but if we can begin to see South Stars, well now the whole thing's ranked in favor of your growth."[7]

One of Peggi's favorite books on this subject is *You Are Not Stuck: How Soul-Guided Choices Transform Fear into Freedom* by Becky Vollmer. Her book highlights the struggle most of us have all experienced between who we want to be, who others think we should be and who we actually are:

> When the voices of Other People drown out the voice of your own intuition, you exist in a state that's out of alignment, beyond your boundaries and inconsistent with what your soul knows is right and true for you…
>
> And remember, a decision to change course doesn't imply that the direction you've headed in all this time was the wrong one—perhaps it served you well for years and years—and, bonus, it brought you to the place where you stand today: wiser, more connected to your evolving spirit, and ready for something different. That's not failure, that's awakening.
>
> The question is, awakening to what?[8]

Like Bell and Vollmer, Peggi has had many South Star experiences that have shown her how she didn't want to be in the world. She has worked with dance studio owner/directors, supervisors, managers, social workers, coaches, teachers, facilitators, writers, and speakers in her career who have shown her who she didn't want to be like and others she aspired to emulate.

Brigitta's South Star Story:

Being a Reiki Master as well as a Life Coach, my business model and my offerings are different from other coaches. This unique approach to healing has helped me to discern my South Stars.

Having taken multiple online and in-person classes, I've evaluated which settings offered the most value to me as a participant. Also, I've examined my own business to determine where my clients flourish the most. And so, my South Star would be offering huge online workshops with unlimited numbers that don't offer any individual coaching or Q&A. Not that there is anything wrong with that approach, but I prefer to work with smaller groups of people. This format supports intimacy and can be a safe environment for those people who tend to hide in large groups. Because of this, my on-line workshops are with small groups of people and only recorded for participants.

There is a downside to this financially; I won't make the big bucks of loading a Zoom call with over fifty people. That's okay, though. My North Star, my values, are connection and contribution. I'm not casting shade or saying that those big offerings aren't wonderful for some people. But for me, to stay en route to my North Star, I don't offer those types of experiences. And as a side note, I no longer participate in them either.

Peggi's South Star Stories:

When I graduated from college, I thought I wanted to be a teacher, so I signed up to be a substitute at our local high school to experience it firsthand. Within the first few months, I knew it wasn't a good fit for me. I loved the teaching part, but I didn't like being in a classroom all day; it felt claustrophobic and restrictive.

I once worked as an aerobics instructor and a tap teacher for a dance studio in the Bay Area where there was great emphasis placed on solo performances, a practice called the "star system." There's nothing wrong with that, but when we moved north, I decided to create a studio that focused on group and teamwork, and everything related to putting on a performance. If students didn't want to dance, they learned marketing, lighting, costume/set/merchandise design, stage managing/directing, and so on. I didn't want students to feel inferior, but to feel a part of something bigger than themselves.

My studio, called "Heart and Sole" had aerobics, tumbling, ballet, tap, jazz, and an art studio. Students ranged in age from three to eighty-three. We had a separate nonprofit that put on The Nutcracker, summer plays, and musicals in partnership with the local school district and community college. Our focus was not on creating stars for competition. Rather, we focused on creating connection, community, and confidence. Students learned life skills. This free-style type of teaching fit my personality much better than the traditional classroom.

Activity 1: Recognizing Your South Stars

Write in your journal for 20-30 minutes about your own South Star experiences/memories.

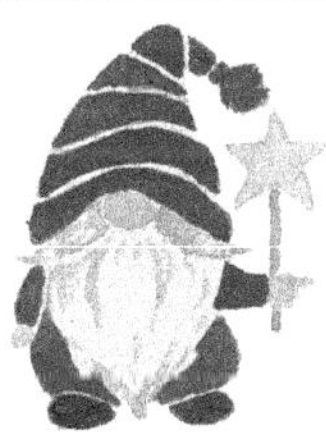

Gnorth suggests: Take some time with this. You may surprise yourself.

Chapter Three

North Stars

"The North Star, with its unwavering light, serves as a timeless reminder of the power and importance of purpose."
-Will Poston

Meditation: Anchor and Connect

Take a deep breath. Either sitting or standing, plant your feet firmly on the ground. Take several deep breaths, following your inhales and exhales.

Visualize the base of your spine. Imagine attached to your tailbone is a long chord with an anchor attached at the end.

With your eyes closed, imagine this anchor dropping through the floor beneath you, into the ground, going deeper and deeper through the layers of dirt, until it reaches the core of the earth. Imagine this long chord being taut but not tight…you are tethered to the center of the earth but can easily sway from side to side. Take a few moments to experience this sensation of being fully grounded and tethered to the earth.

Now imagine another chord reaching up and out from the crown of your head. It's reaching up into the heavens, beyond the sky and the clouds. Feel how these two chords support you in feeling both grounded to this present moment and connected to your higher consciousness… at the same time.

Enjoy this sensation for as long as you like. Utilize this activity when you are feeling ungrounded or stressed.

North Star Defined

Overall, the North Star is a powerful symbol of guidance and direction that has been used throughout history by different cultures. It reminds us to stay true to ourselves and follow our own path, even in the darkest of times. Finding your North Star is a precursor to goal setting and, even more importantly, it's the key to leading a life of meaning and fulfillment.

From The Curious Coach, by Michelle Boxall:

> In the physical sense, the North Star is the anchor of the northern sky. It's a landmark which helps those who follow it determine their direction as it glows brightly to guide them and lead toward a purposeful destination. The earth's axis is pointed almost directly at the North Star. During the course of the night, the North Star doesn't rise or set, it remains in very nearly the same spot above the northern horizon year-round while the other stars circle around it.[9]

With the whistle-stop astronomy bit done, how do we make that work for us on our own journey to a purposeful destination? How could using the metaphor of a North Star help our own discovery of our deepest calling?

Knowing what your own personal North Star is, is basically knowing your life's purpose; what you are here on this earth to do. It's our inner compass; the part of us that knows our passion, purpose, and life direction.

Imagine a fixed point on which you can focus your direction of travel. A point which, despite whatever else goes on around it, stays exactly where it is. Wherever you are, whatever you're doing, whoever you're with, you can recalibrate yourself by fixing your sights back on your North Star.

Everyone's North Star is deeply personal to them. Some examples might be, writing a book, climbing Mount Everest, owning a business, volunteering at an orphanage in Africa or walking the Camino de Santiago in Europe.

Gnora reminds: There is no right or wrong here because it's yours and yours only. No one gets to tell you what it should be.

Austin Bollinger puts it this way: "We all have dreams, goals, or ambitions because we envision a better future for ourselves. Sure, you may love life and appreciate everything you have right this very moment, but I'd bet you also have something you want to build towards in your future."

Ask yourself: What do you want your life to look like? What do you hope to achieve? Do you want to travel the world? Write a book? Run a marathon? Go back to school? Open up a dog-grooming business? Change careers? Create a non-profit? Awesome! Set goals that build towards that.

Get curious, ask yourself:

- What brings you joy?
- What do you get excited about?
- What puts a huge grin on your face?
- What is *the* most important thing you want to achieve?
- What activities make you lose track of time?
- What are you naturally good at or deeply curious about?
- What do people often come to you for help with?
- Ask yourself what you truly want, not what you think you should want.

Which leads us to another crucial question: WHY?

- Why does this goal put a huge grin on your face?
- What is it that resonates so strongly for you that you can call it your North Star?

Before settling on your North Star, let's find more clarity. Let's start with what drives our own behaviors.

- Why do you do what you do?
- Why do you want what you want?
- Why do you value things differently than others?

The quick answer: you do what you do to FEEL A CERTAIN WAY.

Knowing what drives you to do what you do is the most potent form of clarity you have. This information is a goldmine for you to efficiently identify and achieve your goals.

Gnorth adds: Memory lane can be magical! Don't worry if some memories seem 'too small' or silly. Often our most profound insights come from the simplest moments of joy.

ACTIVITY 1: Favorite Memories

(The following exercise is an adapted mashup of two exercises created by Mastin Kipp and Daniel LaPorte.)[10] [11]

Step One

Turn to your journal and write about 10 to 15 of your favorite memories. These can be as recent as yesterday or span all the way back to your childhood. Take at least 15 to 30 minutes to compile this list. This can be fun because our brains are evolutionarily wired to remember the negative memories more than the positive ones. This is a "feel good" activity.

Here are some questions to support you in remembering your favorite memories:

- What classes have you loved?
- Travels?
- People?
- What did you love doing when you were a child? With who?
- What has made your heart sing?
- What about those times when you completely lost track of time…what were you doing?
- When have you felt happiest?
- When have you felt completely aligned? When have you felt most "like yourself"?

You don't need to write out the whole scenario because they are your memories. Just write a quick "heading" for each memory. List 10 to 15 of your favorite memories.

Some memories from Brigitta's list:

- Trip to Africa
- Retreat on Vashon Island
- Retreat I hosted last summer
- That pizza party sleepover with Fran in 4th grade
- Co-writing/producing/starring in the short film, "Stalkers"

(I don't need to go into detail about my trip to Africa or the pizza party in 4th grade because I remember them vividly.)

Peggi's list:

- Floating down the Tuolumne River with my dad in Yosemite National Park
- Going with my mom to City of Paris Department Store to see the multi-story Christmas tree
- When my children were born
- Owning/Directing a dance/aerobics/performing arts studio
- Teaching social work

Step Two

Next to each memory, write out how you felt during that experience. What feelings and or values does this memory evoke in you as you think of it?

Excitement? Accomplishment? Liberation? Security? Love? Acceptance? Empowerment? A sense of Connection? A sense of Vitality? A sense of Peace?

Write out your feelings/values next to these memories. You will likely see repetition. The same feelings/values will likely be repeated. That is okay; it's supposed to happen that way.

Step Three

Compile a list of the top 3 to 5 feelings you wrote.

Brigitta's top 3 feelings based on the above exercise: Connection, Contribution, Creative Expression.

Some memories from Brigitta's list:

- Trip to Africa **Connection**
- Retreat on Vashon Island **Connection**
- Retreat I hosted last summer **Connection, Creative Expression**
- That pizza party sleepover with Fran in 4th grade **Connection**
- Co-writing/producing/starring in the short film, "Stalkers" **Creative Expression, Contribution**

Peggi's top 5 feelings: Connection, Freedom, Love, Creativity, Humor

Some memories from Peggi's list:

- Floating down the Tuolumne River with my dad in Yosemite National Park **Connection, Freedom**
- Going with my mom to City of Paris Department Store to see the multi-story Christmas tree **Curiosity, Connection, Creativity**

- When my children were born **Love, Connection**
- Owning/Directing a dance/aerobics/performing arts studio **Creativity, Connection**
- Teaching social work **Creativity, Connection, Humor**

Peggi's ed note: This was so interesting for me, as the feelings/values I attached are four of my core values from Chapter One: love, connection, curiosity, integrity, and humor. Did you have the same experience?

Brigitta's ed note: Me too. I keep returning to Connection, Contribution, and feeling safe to express my creativity.

Spend some time thinking about these feelings/values and see if you can rate which of these feelings is **most important** to you. In other words, when you feel most "like yourself", which of these feelings are you experiencing the most?

Congratulations, you have just discovered your personal GPS system. As long as your goals elicit these feelings, you are in alignment with your North Star.

If the thought of achieving your goals doesn't light you up like these favorite memories, then your goals are not in alignment with your true desires. And because of this, you will lack the motivation and energy required to achieve those goals. Make sure that you are honest in that the goals you set for yourself are your goals, not someone else's. If, however, the journey to achieving your goals elicits those yummy, juicy feelings you just honed in on, then you are unstoppable.

Activity 2: Write Your Own Obituary

Writing your own obituary is a powerful exercise in self-reflection, and it connects deeply with the idea of finding your North Star because it forces you to confront what truly matters in your life. Elliott Appel, CFP (Kindness Financial Planning) asks this, "What better way to figure out how to live your ideal life than to work backwards?"

Ask yourself: What do you want to be remembered for? What kind of legacy would make you proud? What contributions did you make?

By doing this activity, you might realize that your current path doesn't reflect the life you want to be remembered for. That insight can be a catalyst for change.

Appel suggests:

You can write it in the first or third person. I'm partial to the first person. It's different. How often do you see an obituary written in first person?

Depending on who you are as a person or who you want to become, you have a few routes to take with writing your own obituary.

You could make your obituary funny throughout. You could make it heartwarming. You could make it primarily heartwarming with touches of humor. You could stick to the facts with sprinkles of stories.

The best obituaries tell stories. They paint a picture of a human being who is no longer with us. They bring the person to life.[12]

Activity 3: Landing on Your North Star

What you value and aspire to. In your journal, follow these prompts:
Identity your long-term passions:

- What matters most to you?
- What activities energize you most?

Envision the outcome:

- Is your North Star a change, contribution or achievement or a combination of all three?
- If we were flies on the wall, what would we see you doing?

Get clear on your "why":

- Start with your why. Comedian Michael Jr. says this: "How do I know what I'm supposed to do? The question you should really ask is 'Why am I here?' Because if you know your why, your what becomes more clear and more impactful. My what is I am a comedian. My why is to inspire people to walk in purpose."

Express your North Star compellingly:

- Avoid buzzwords that are vague and look like the posters you see on business walls like these:

Be the Best Version of Yourself
Trust the Process
Just be You

These kinds of quotes are what you see on Pinterest boards. They often contained images such as fog, horses, rainbows, and sunsets (insert snoring emoji). They come across as vague, boring and without action.

Write your North Star Mission Statement:

Peggi's North Star Mission Statement

"To become the healthiest, most informed, and authentic version of myself—mind, body, and soul, so that I can inspire others to believe in their own worth and potential, and create spaces where people feel seen, heard, and empowered."

Brigitta's North Star Mission Statement

"To contribute to the growth of others by both embodying and sharing the healing energy of Reiki - to live my life as an example of how this alternative healing modality can be a normal part of one's health care and spiritual practice."

You did it! Part One is Done!

Before moving on, take some time to reflect on all the work you have done. Notice which activities were really fun and easy for you. Also, take note of the exercises you resisted doing. Which ones did you skip altogether? Why?

The reason for asking these questions is not to punish ourselves but to encourage curiosity and self-compassion. Both of those qualities—curiosity and compassion, are necessary for lasting growth and change to occur.

So, have a loving "check in" before tackling Part 2.

Gnorth and Gnora remind us that there is no need to rush. There is no "cosmic timekeeper" watching over you. Take all the time you need to enjoy the nuggets of gold you may have excavated so far.

PART TWO

NORTH STAR GOALS AND STRATEGIES

Your North Star is the why. Goals and strategies are the how. Without them, your vision remains abstract. Goals give you tangible milestones, and strategies provide the roadmap to reach them.

Life is full of distractions. Goals help you filter out the noise and stay aligned with what truly matters. Strategies ensure your actions are consistent with your values. Goals allow you to track how far you've come. They help you celebrate wins and reflect on setbacks—both of which are crucial for personal growth.

Strategies are flexible. As life changes, they help you pivot without losing sight of your North Star. This keeps you resilient and intentional even in uncertain times. When faced with choices, your goals and strategies act as a compass. They help you ask: Does this move me closer to my North Star?

As you move through this section of the workbook, we have provided several ways to identify your North Star goals and strategies. Pick the ones that resonate and leave the ones that don't.

Chapter Four

Goal Setting Tools:

Future Tripping, WOOP & Contingency Plans

"The secret of change is to focus all of your energy, not on fighting the old, but on building the new."
-Socrates

Meditation: Plunge and Stabilize

Take a deep breath. Either sitting or standing, plant your feet firmly on the ground. Take several deep breaths, following your inhales and exhales.

Trusting your instincts, imagine the space around you. If you were to examine the energy field surrounding you, what color is it? Is it clear? Or is it murky? Is there debris floating by? Is it stormy and turbulent?

If the energy around you feels anything other than clear and serene, do this plunging technique.

Imagine you and your energy field are in a large clear glass French Press coffee pot. Above you is a plunger that will soon descend and clear any and all non-beneficial energy. Take a deep breath in and allow the plunger to begin its magic. Feel the plunger clear your energy as it descends. Starting with the space above your head, visualize it squeezing out any unwanted murkiness… it clears everything all the way down to your toes.

Once the plunger has cleared your energy, imagine all that gunk as a puddle just below you. Visualize that pool of debris quickly seeping straight down into the earth where it can be transformed.

How do you feel?

You may wish to repeat this meditation several times until you feel cleared of any non-beneficial energies.

Building the Fantasy to Fine-Tune Our Goals.

Let's future trip together. Now that you have landed on your North Star, it's time to picture and plan your route to get there. In these next chapters, we offer a charcuterie tray of strategies and tools to reach your destination. Here we offer you two tools, Future Tripping and WOOP, followed by the creation of a contingency plan.

Future Tripping Explained

Future tripping can be a creative tool when used intentionally. Imagining future scenarios helps you visualize the life you want to live, explore different paths toward your purpose and clarify long-term goals that align with your values. Just like writing your obituary, future tripping can help you ask: "If I want to be there in 10 years, what do I need to do now?" This backward planning is a practical way to align your current actions with your North Star.

Imagining a future where you're living your purpose can create a strong emotional anchor. That feeling can help you stay committed when things get hard. And they will.

Getting this specific with your vision helps you see your roadmap more clearly. This process helps you identify exactly what you need to learn, who could help you, what you might eliminate, and what you want to cultivate. This is how you can start to write an action plan to achieve your goal.

Gnorth says future tripping should feel like the best daydream ever! If visualizing your goal feels like work, you might be trying too hard. Let your imagination run wild and have fun with it.

Activity 1: Future Tripping

Close your eyes and envision yourself achieving your goal, i.e., see yourself holding your printed book, doing the book signing, posing for pics with fans, going on podcast interviews, etc. Get really specific:

- Notice what you ARE doing and what you are NOT doing.
- Who is there with you? Who is NOT there with you?
- What new skills have you learned along the way?
- What behaviors have become habits and which ones have you eliminated?

Spend 15 minutes fantasizing and fully associating with all the things that are happening in this future visualization. (This should feel fantastic, by the way!)

Then, put your thoughts in your journal. Let it be messy. Free flowing. When you are finished, go back and read all the information you just received from your future self.

Now ask yourself, "How can you turn this "future trip" into a reality?"

Jot down anything that comes to mind that you could do, now, to start bringing this future into your reality today. Again, let it be messy. Don't get hung up on the "how", just get all the ideas out of your head and onto the page. You will use this information later when you are brainstorming how to plot your journey towards your North Star.

Austin Bollinger, author of *Crush Your Goals* writes,

> As human beings, we're incredibly emotional. Our emotions can cause us to fall in love in a moment's notice, buy things we don't need at the drop of a hat, help a total stranger in need, or even quit a job in a ball of fire on a bad day – the list goes on and on.[13]

How emotionally attached are you to your goals?

Do they excite you? Float your boat?

Have you ever heard of SMART goals? Specific, Measurable, Achievable, Relevant and Time Specific. But what if your goals punch all five of those boxes, but they don't contribute to a brighter future, or get you excited to jump out of bed, or provide significance to your life?

What if the SMART goal acronym helps you set a bunch of goals that you don't really care about – like not even one iota? Trust us, we have tried that many times only to find out we didn't really have much of an emotional attachment to the goals we set.

To determine whether we are really emotionally attached to the goal, we need to ask the following questions:

- What do you want your life to look like?
- What do you hope to achieve? For example: Do you want to travel the world? Set goals that build towards that. Do you want to start your own nonprofit organization? That's outstanding!
- Do you have an emotional attachment to the goal?
- What would the goal look like once it has been achieved?
- Most importantly, how do the goals you set tie to your North Star?

Gnora suggests: Set goals that require you to learn new skills or go for challenges that previously intimidated you. We learn best right outside our comfort zone.

WOOP, there it is ...

One of Peggi's favorite goal-setting tools is a fun little strategy called WOOP. The WOOP method of goal setting uses all of the above questions and prepares you for the obstacles that may get in your way.

WOOP is a science-based mental strategy that you can use to find and fulfill your North Star/ Purpose. Based on Gabriele Oettinger's 20 years of research in the science of motivation, WOOP presents a unique and surprising idea: The obstacles that we think most impede us from fulfilling our wishes can actually help us to realize them. WOOP instructs us to dream our future dreams but then to imagine what obstacles inside ourselves prevent us from achieving those dreams. In research studies, WOOP has helped people reduce stress and increase work engagement, find integrative solutions to problems, and improve time management. It has supported adults in losing weight, drinking less alcohol, and sustaining healthier relationships. Children and adolescents using WOOP improved school attendance, as well as effort and achievement in school.[14]

Activity 2: WOOP It Up!

W is for WISH:

- What is an important wish that you want to accomplish in the next ________ (time period)?
- Bumper-sticker it up. 3-6 words.
- Hardest part of WOOP…landing on the wish. (North Star/purpose)

For example, One of Peggi's North Stars is to write a book to identify and reduce the effects of Secondary Traumatic Stress in the helping fields. My bumper sticker? "Down With STS"

O is for OUTCOME:

- What would be the best thing, the best outcome of fulfilling your wish? How would fulfilling your wish make you feel? Close your eyes and take a few minutes to really see it, feel it, and imagine it. Hold it in your mind.

Peggi's outcome would be that fewer people would turn to unhealthy habits such as alcohol, eating disorders, substance misuse, strained relationships, burnout. They would be happier in their jobs, and there would be greater outcomes for the people they serve.

O is for OBSTACLE:

- What is it within you that holds you back from fulfilling your wish? What is your inner obstacle? It might be an emotion, an irrational belief or a habit. What is it? Dig a little deeper. Close your eyes and hold it in your mind.
- If it's a goal you've made before, but haven't accomplished, what got in the way?
- If it's a new goal, play out any scenarios that you believe will get in the way of
- your achieving your goals.

Peggi's obstacles include making time to research and write, and internally having imposter syndrome: "Am I even qualified to write on the subject? Who am I to write a book?" (We will addressed this very important subject of imposter syndrome in Chapter Ten.)

P is for PLAN:

- What can you do to overcome your obstacle? Name an effective action you can take or an effective thought you can think to overcome your obstacle.
- If________ [obstacle happens] then I will ________.

Peggi's plans are to set specific times for writing and research and to reframe negative self-talk and say affirmations like "I know this subject. My lived experience is valuable. What I have to say is important."

Obstacles Call for Contingency Plans

Contingency plans are alternative courses of action that you can take if your original plan is disrupted by unforeseen events or circumstances. No matter how well you plan, unexpected challenges will arise. Having a contingency or backup plan allows you to keep moving forward rather than stalling. Think of it like this: If your GPS route is closed, a contingency plan is your alternative route—it keeps you moving toward your destination.

Sometimes, we can predict the future. Just go to any family gathering around the holidays and you can easily predict who will have too much to drink, who will say something embarrassing, who will have their feelings hurt, and who will vow never to host it again. Right?

Preparing ahead and having a plan for these predictable challenges helps build flexibility and resilience.

Writing a contingency plan for potential obstacles is now being utilized by patients recovering from hip replacement surgery. Patients are advised to write out a plan ahead of time for that moment they will want to quit or not show up for physical therapy. Then, when their resistance does come up, they are prepared. This preparation means they can predict this issue and therefore conquer it more easily. Studies have shown that people who plan ahead to avoid their excuses are more likely to have a faster recovery.

Activity 3: Write a Contingency Plan

Take a few minutes right now to create a contingency plan wherever possible.
What obstacles can I predict? How can I plan for them now?
What about personal, internal obstacles?
When might I get stuck, feel overwhelmed, want to shut down, etc?

You can use this template to create your contingency plan:

1. North Star Goal: Description
2. Key Milestones: List major steps or achievements that lead toward you North Star.
3. Potential Risks & Challenges
4. Contingency Actions

Gnorth reminds us: Preparing for what could go wrong, saves us precious energy by eliminating excess worry.

Brigitta's Contingency Plan for navigating social events while remaining alcohol free: Socializing without the "liquid courage" of alcohol can be a major hurdle for many people. Planning ahead can be a game-changing strategy for navigating these events while remaining sober.

My contingency plan included what to order at the bar (mocktails if possible, sparkling water if not.) I also armed myself with my responses to people should they notice and/or comment on the fact that I was not drinking alcohol. I also made sure to check in with my support group both before and after the event for accountability and moral support.

Because I was prepared, the events quickly became easier and easier to handle. Now, I don't even need to prepare. But having a fully fleshed out contingency plan helped me stay on track in those early days of sobriety.

Peggi's Contingency Plan is similar to Brigitta's. When I first stopped drinking alcohol, I did these things: brought my own non-alcoholic beverages; carried my own glass with said non-alcoholic beverages so that no one could put a boozy one in my hand. I drove my own car so I could leave when I needed or wanted to and ultimately chose not to go anywhere where alcohol was the main event.

Chapter Five

Small Wins/Big Outcomes

"The elevator to success is broken. You'll have to use the stairs…one step at a time."
-Jo Gerrard

Meditation: Expansion/Zooming Out

Take a deep breath. Either sitting or standing, plant your feet firmly on the ground. Take several deep breaths paying close attention to your inhales and exhales.

Look around the space you are in. Notice two things that are close to you. You might notice your hands, your feet, etc. Take an inhale and exhale doing nothing but noticing these two things.

Now, notice two things a little further away. Maybe you notice the window in front of you or the carpet by the door. Take an inhale and exhale noticing only those two things.

Next, zoom out further. Can you notice what is outside the window or imagine what's on the other side of the door? Can you hear things? Smell things? Take an inhale and exhale and notice only those few things.

Continue noticing only a few things, each time expanding out further and further. Do this for a minute.

Do you notice how all of these things are existing in this present moment? You can choose which to focus on at any given moment. (This is a fantastic mindfulness technique to use when you are feeling overwhelmed.)

Lifting Up Small Wins

The saying, "There's only one way to eat an elephant, one bite at a time" is a metaphor that means you tackle big, overwhelming tasks by breaking them down into smaller, manageable steps. It's often used to encourage persistence and patience when facing something that feels too large or difficult to handle all at once—like a big project, a life challenge or long-term goal. The Japanese have a name for this strategy that relies on tiny, continuing improvements to create change. It's called "Kaisen." We call these small wins.

With all the people Brigitta has worked with both as a coach and a Pilates instructor, the people who take daily baby steps towards their goals have a better chance of actually achieving their goals. In fact, most successful people don't kill themselves trying to do a ton every day. They take small, effective bite-sized actions consistently.

Many of us have heard this before yet aren't following this time-proven advice. We still think great big goals require great big actions. But the truth is, rarely is anything in life "one big action." It's usually a string of small accomplishments that leads to the big accomplishment or goal.

For example, let's consider running a marathon. You will need to train for this goal. Brigitta can attest to that! Having run one herself, she can tell you her training consisted of a LOT of smaller runs: "The training group I ran with started with a ONE-mile run. That's it! We ran one mile together and ran one mile again on our own twice that week. The next week, we ran two miles together with additional short runs on our own. Then we ran three miles, then four… eventually, we ran an entire 26 mile run together two weeks before the actual marathon."

Ask any writer how they wrote their book or script? They will probably tell you they started with an outline and then plugged away at it daily. They didn't write the book in a weekend. Books are written one day at a time. Mark Manson, author of The Subtle Art of Giving A F*ck, set time aside every day to write at least 200 crappy words a day, beginning with an outline, listening to music, and drinking lots of caffeine.

James Clear, author of Atomic Habits, writes:

> Success is the product of daily habits—not once-in-a-lifetime transformations…Just as money multiplies through compound interest, the effects of your habits multiply as you repeat them daily. Small, consistent actions -doing a little better each day - are the real secret to long-term success. [15]

So then, how can we make these small steps transformational? By systemizing these bite-size actions. Take a look at these small steps and see if they can be a repeated pattern of behavior. To use the examples above, notice how the goals of writing a book and running a marathon were actually turned into a system of behavior. Writers write (almost every day). Runners run (almost every day). Can you turn your small actions into repeatable steps that, if continued diligently, could lead you to your North Star?

Gnora says: Remember: Baby steps still count as steps! A tiny action taken consistently will always beat a giant leap taken once. Progress is progress, no matter how small it looks.

Brigitta's Example:

Back in the early 90's I wanted to move to Los Angeles to further my acting career. The biggest obstacle (and believe me, there were many!) was getting a green card. If I couldn't legally work in the U.S., there was no point in moving there. My first step was to seek legal support to obtain a working visa. My (expensive) attorney immediately put me to work on "building my case."

My biggest asset was the fact that the show I was starring in was international. That meant I could potentially show proof of worldwide press. She wanted me to gather all the magazines and print media I could possibly find.

The Internet did not exist then. I had to call or write (snail mail) magazine and newspaper editors to ask for copies of any stories they had run about our show. Then, after they arrived, I had to go to the stationery store to photocopy all of those articles and pictures. This was a LOT of work. I avoided feeling overwhelmed by only doing a little bit EVERY DAY. I plugged away at this goal for six months and eventually had enough press for her to build my case.

It worked—I got my green card and moved to LA later that year.

Peggi's example: Writing my book, This Side of Alcohol.

On the first day of my alcohol-free life, I began journaling my feelings. Even if I just wrote a sentence or a quote, I wrote every single day. For the first year, I posted my entries on social media, and after the first year, I posted weekly. At the end of two years, I had the foundation for a book that I published in 2021. Six years and many filled journals later, I am still writing daily. Journaling has become a non-negotiable part of my morning routine.

Gnora encourages you to reflect on this strategy every few weeks. Pretty soon you'll see you are accomplishing more than you expected! And that enthusiasm breeds more inspired actions.

Activity 1: Small Wins Journal Prompts

- What are some small actions that I can take towards your North Star Goals?
- How can I "systemize" these actions and turn them into habits?
- If I could accomplish one small thing today, what would it be?
- What's one reason this small step matters to me?
- How will I feel after completing this step?

Chapter Six

Redefining Success: The Goal Attainment Rating Scale

"If I am going to fall, fall forward."
-Denzel Washington

Meditation: Pick a Sense

Pick any sense and spend two minutes examining it fully.

For example, the sense of sound.

Is there a hum of electricity where you are?
Is there a sound in your ears?
Can you hear your pulse?
Can you hear a neighbor's TV?
Can you hear traffic?
Can you hear other people talking?
Can you hear a dog barking?
Can you hear wind blowing outside?
Can you hear the ocean?

Notice what you are sensing and experience it as if it were the first time you have ever felt it before.

Goal Attainment Rating Scale (GARS)

The Goal Attainment Rating Scale (GARS) method and the concept of a North Star are both powerful tools for inspirational growth—and they complement each other beautifully. GARS helps you translate your North Star into concrete, trackable goals because it helps you define what success looks like at different levels.

You can regularly assess how close you are to your North Star by evaluating the attainment of smaller goals using the GARS scale. GARS makes your progress toward your North Star transparent. By reviewing GARS scores, you can reflect on what's working, what's not, and how to recalibrate your path toward your North Star.

GARS is a five-point rating scale. The middle point on the scale corresponds to the expected learning outcome. For example, "I want to complete a quilt for my son's birthday on December 4 (six months from now)." This would be considered the most realistic/likely outcome to a goal. The higher and lower points on the scale simply indicate whether you achieved more success than expected, or less.

We don't always meet our goals 100% of the time, and sometimes we exceed them. GARS gives room for both, and we can feel like we have made progress even when life gets "lifey." Think of GARS as a stepping stone towards your North Star. Tracking it with GARS helps you stay focused, measure impact, and adjust your approach as needed.

Activity 2: Practicing GARS[16]

While you are filling out your GARS, ask yourself the following questions and include in your rating sheet:

- What will be different about your life if you reach this goal? What will success look like?
- How will you know if you've reached this goal?
- How do you want to feel? (It's not about the goal itself. For example, making a quilt for my my son will make me proud, knowing how much handmade things mean to him
- What excites you about this goal? (You may find out that this particular goal doesn't light you up, and that's good information too.)

Gnorth adds: GARS is like having a flexible measuring tape instead of a rigid ruler. Life rarely goes exactly as planned, and that's okay! Success comes in many sizes and shapes.

GARS Example: Peggi

Vision/Dream/Wish: I want to complete my Hawaiian print pineapple quilt for my son Brett by his birthday.

Scale Value	Description of level rating
Much More Than Expected	I will make two of the pillows that come with the pattern.
Somewhat More Than Expected	I will complete the quilt two months before Brett's birthday.
Expected Level Of Outcome	I will have the quilt finished by Brett's birthday. Hawaii is my happy place. I bought most of the fabric in Maui, and it will remind me of my trips there. This project pushes me out of my comfort zone because the callenging pattern is at least one level up in difficulty, and I will feel quite accomplished. This will be a legacy project to leave for my son and connects to my core value of creativity.
Somewhat Less Than Expected	I will complete the quilt top and have it ready to send off to my long-arm quilter, who will attach the batting and quilt back.
Much Less Than Expected	I will have all the quilt pieces cut out, and some of the blocks will be sewn together.

GARS Example: Brigitta

Vision/Dream/Wish: To be featured in "*Reiki News Magazine*"

Scale Value	Description of level rating
Much More Than Expected	Reiki News offers me a contract to be a regular contributors to their magazine.
Somewhat More Than Expected	Not only do the accept my article, they include my artwork and make it three pages.
Expected Level Of Outcome	Within 60 days, I will write an article about being a Fusion Energy/ Creative Teacher and submit to Reiki News Magazine, which will be accepted and appear in their summer edition. This would be a huge win for my business. I will feel pride and feel the validation that comes from being recognized by a respected, professional trade magazine. And, this will fulfill my core value of contribution.
Somewhat Less Than Expected	The magazine editor likes my article, but wants some rewrites, and I miss the first deadline.
Much Less Than Expected	I submit the article and get a lot of positive feedback. However, the editor doesn't think it's a fit for the summer issue and asks me to resubmit later in the year.

Your GARS

Vision/Dream/Wish:

Scale Value	Description of level rating
Much More Than Expected	
Somewhat More Than Expected	
Expected Level Of Outcome	
Somewhat Less Than Expected	
Much Less Than Expected	

Chapter Seven

Ready. Set. Action: Acting 101

"Pretending is not just play. Pretending is imagined possibility. Pretending, or acting, is a very valuable life skill and we do it all the time." -Meryl Streep

Meditation: Take a Snapshot (or a Polaroid...we're dating ourselves...)

You can do this sitting or standing.

Close your eyes and take 2 deep breaths.

Take a quick scan of your body and notice where your attention goes. Allow your intuition to reveal whatever part of your body wants to be observed. Once you have placed your focus there, imagine taking a "snapshot" of this area. For example, maybe you are holding tension in your neck and shoulders, or maybe you are noticing that your feet are cold. Notice where your attention goes (i.e., your neck or feet) and then imagine taking a snapshot of this part.

Now imagine light pouring into this place in your body. Notice how this area is being completely drenched in light.

Then, when you feel like its fully saturated, allow for the light to evaporate like steam.

Notice what has changed with this place in your body.

Take another snapshot.

Check in with this part throughout the day. Compare how you're feeling in those moments with your mental "snapshot". Revisit this quick activity as needed.

Ready. Set. Action.

The preparation skills actors use are not that different from the steps we take when pursuing our North Star. Actors analyze their scenes and make decisions on how to "play the role" based on their character's desires, obstacles, etc. So, let's look at your North Star through the lens of a camera and make you the star of your own life.

When actors start to work on a script, their first step is to get a clear idea of what motivates their character. Their first task is to ask themselves:

- What is my character's overriding intention/motivation?
- What makes them tick?
- What do they love and what do they hate? What are their core values?
- When are they most powerful, and what are their weaknesses?
- Why are they in this script and what role do they play in the telling of this story?

In other words, what is their North Star? How committed are they to pursuing their desires? And, what could derail their intentions?

From there, an actor will get specific. They will continue to examine every single scene where their character appears. Their analysis of each of these scenes starts with these three components:

1. What does my character want in this scene? This is known as their "Objective". Specifically, what is motivating them to say what they are saying and do what they are doing? What do they WANT to get, have happen, etc?

2. What are their obstacles? What is stopping them from getting what they want? Are these obstacles internal? Psychological? External? Other people?

3. How are they going to overcome those obstacles and get what they want? What tactics will they use to achieve their goals?

Sound familiar? This is the same way you are charting your journey to your North Star. For a Hollywood story to be good, we want our hero to be committed to achieving their goals despite their inner and outer adversaries. For that same story to be great, we want to see our hero do whatever it takes to achieve their goals AND be courageous and creative in how they overcome all their obstacles.

Gnora says you're already the star of your own life story! The only difference is now you get to be a more intentional actor instead of just winging it.

Activity 1: Break Down a Scene

Pick a scene that you love from any movie or TV show. Watch this scene, asking yourself the following questions:

- What is the hero's motivation in the scene?
- What are their obstacles?
- How are they trying to overcome their obstacles?
- Bonus question: Why do you love this scene so much?

Activity 2: Cast Yourself as the Lead

Think for a moment about a potential issue or obstacle that may arise in the near future. Imagine this upcoming challenge as a scene in a movie. Cast yourself as the lead (the hero) and analyze this situation as if it were a scene from a film.

- What is your motivation in this scene? Hint…what is your goal?
- What are your obstacles? Are they internal? (Imposter Syndrome, Chapter Ten)
- Are they external? (i.e. You need time, money, or support)
- How are you going to overcome these obstacles? (Contingency Plans, Chapter Five)

Peggi Cooney and Brigitta Dau

Chapter Eight

Less is More: The 80/20 Principle: Underwhelming Our Way to Success

"Simplicity is not a destination, but a journey. I t's about constantly refining and prioritizing what truly matters."
-author unknown

Meditation: Notice the Pause

Take a deep breath. Either sitting or standing, plant your feet firmly on the ground. Take several deep breaths, following your inhales and exhales.

Next, notice the pause at the end of your exhale.

Notice the pause at the end of your inhale.

See if you can elongate the pause on both the inhales and the exhales.

Do this for one minute, then return to regular breathing. Notice the pauses as they naturally occur.

The 80/20 Principle

The 80/20 Principle—also known as the Pareto Principle—states that 80% of outcomes come from 20% of efforts. When applied to your North Star, it becomes a powerful lens for focus, alignment and impact. The 80/20 principle helps you identify the 20% of actions, habits, or relationships that contribute to reaching your North Star. This principle helps you cut out the noise and maximize your energy and joy.

According to time management guru Brian Tracy and Italian economist Vilfredo Pareto, 20% of your customers will account for 80% of your sales. 20% of your products will account for 80% of your profit.[17]This means that it's important to choose your goals wisely. Since 20% of your actions generate 80% of your achievements, focusing on those key actions is essential for success and needs to be identified.

But don't take our word for it. Let's look at a wildly successful company we all know:

> Apple. Remember Apple in the early 2000s? The company had dozens of products—printers, digital cameras, multiple variations of computers—and it was struggling. When Steve Jobs returned, he slashed the product line by nearly 70%, famously saying, "We're going to focus on four things." Instead of spreading their energy thinly across dozens of offerings, Apple concentrated on the small handful of products that had the greatest potential for impact.

That decision changed everything.

Those few products—the iMac, the PowerBook, and eventually the iPod—became the 20% that generated the vast majority of Apple's momentum, identity, and revenue. By simplifying, streamlining, and doubling down on what mattered most, Apple got back on course to become one of the most influential companies in the world.

They are still utilizing this strategy. The next time you're in your car, notice the billboards you see from Apple. What are they promoting? One thing: iPhones.

How do you apply this principle to the daily actions you take towards your goals?

Activity 1: What's your 20%?

Pull out your "to-do" list or mentally recall what's on it. Circle or mark **three** items that feel:

- most important
- most aligned with your values
- most likely to move your life forward
- most nourishing to your well-being

These are your potential 20%

Gnorth reminds us: Getting out of our habitual thinking can sometimes "free up" time we didn't realize we were wasting. Take a moment to brainstorm different ways to accomplish your tasks.

Chapter Nine

Writing your "Order" to the Universe

"It never fails. The Universe often has a better imagination than we do."
-Ann Dowsett Johnston/Author of "Drink"

Meditation: Cutting thc Chord, Strengthening the Ties

Take a deep breath. Either sitting or standing, plant your feet firmly on the ground. Take several deep breaths, paying close attention to your inhales and exhales.

Visualize yourself surrounded by a clear, effervescent bubble. Imagine strings of energy flowing out from this orb. Notice if these strands are connecting to anything outside of you.

Are these strands floating freely? Are they connecting to the heavens or a higher energy field? Are they connected to something you no longer wish to be connected to? Do these strings feel stale? Are there things around you that you want to be released from? Are you feeling drained by them?

Envision the unwanted chords dissolving and melting away. Envision the strands falling away without any effort.

Also, notice the strengthening of the chords you wish to keep. Feel yourself more firmly tethered to what feels supportive while releasing what no longer serves you.

Take a few deep breaths and allow this visualization to complete itself.

When you feel free and supported, open your eyes.

Asking the Universe for What You Want

By now you have a very clear picture of what your North Star is. You have clarity about what you want and why. You may even have some action plans and contingency plans written up. At the very least, you have a clear North Star Mission Statement that resonates with you and starts you on your path (see Chapter Three).

It's time to add a little magic into this process! If you believe in magic (and if you're reading this, then you probably do) it's time to harness your subconscious mind. It's time to "place your order" with the Universe.

If a cosmic waitress came up to you to take your order, what would you request? Think for a minute about when you order anything in a restaurant or coffee shop. You are usually very specific, right? "Do you want regular 2% milk or rice milk? Which sides do you prefer with your entree? Do you want a cup or a bowl of soup? Do you want your dressing on the side?"

There is a trap many of us have fallen into when stating our desires. This is the snare of "settling for scraps" (i.e. only asking for what we hopefully can get) versus really owning what we WANT. This shows up when we hear ourselves say, "hopefully", or "maybe", or "if it all works out" … These are not empowering statements.

When it comes to desires and intention setting, Brigitta encourages people to "want it like you mean it and state it like you mean it." Unabashedly request your desires and be specific about how you want them to unfold.

Of course, we all know we don't have total control over this. But what if you could conjure up exactly what you wanted? What would be the best-case scenario? Your ideal outcome is what you want to aim your arrow towards. Focusing directly on what you want is how you open yourself up to potential magic. What we focus on expands. What we water grows. Your unapologetic desire is your bulls-eye order from the Universe.

Order like you mean it, says Gnorth. The universe can't deliver what you're afraid to ask for. Be specific, be bold, and remember—you deserve good things!

Activity 1: Order UP!

Dear Universe,

I WANT ____.

I ALSO WANT ____.

WITH THAT I ALSO WANT ________________________________.

AND I WANT _____________________ WITH _________________.

With gratitude,

Your signature here: ______________________________

Activity 2: Rewrite the Above Letter as a "Thank You" Letter to the Universe.

For example:

Dear Universe,
I WANT to be hired as a fitness instructor at my local gym.

Rewritten as a "thank you" letter:

Dear Universe,
Thank you for this amazing opportunity! I have been hired at the Gold's Gym nearest to my house. I'm teaching classes there every week, and I love the members and the staff.

Activity 3: Noticing Your Resistance.

If you are feeling resistant to asking for what you want, let's dig into that with compassion.

Questions to answer in your journal:

Who told you your wishes weren't valid? Do you still agree with them?
Did you create a belief that your desires didn't matter? When?
Why might you have decided that dimming your light was the best option?
Do you feel it's best to stifle your magic? What could happen if you stopped stifling your magic?
What could happen if you let go of all of these beliefs?

Please be gentle with yourself as you excavate these buried beliefs.

Part Two is Done! Pause, and take a deep breath!

Phew! There was a LOT in part two! Take a moment to pat yourself on the back for getting this far. Congratulate yourself on digging deep and cultivating courage. This is a lovely time to "press pause" and reflect on your journey so far.

Carve out some quiet time to journal and reflect on your insights, your "aha's" and all the wins you've had along the way.

Both Gnora and Gnorth think this is a great time to give yourself a gold star or a sticker of your choice.

PART THREE

STAYING THE COURSE

Watching out for obstacles to staying the course of your North Star is crucial because even the most meaningful path can be derailed if you're not mindful. Without noticing, you might start making choices that slowly pull you away from your values and purpose. This "drift" often happens subtly—through habits, distractions, or external pressures.

Obstacles test how deeply you're committed to your North Star. Whether it's fear, doubt, or burnout, these challenges can make you question your direction—unless you're vigilant and prepared to face them. Life throws curveballs—unexpected responsibilities, relationships, or opportunities. If you're not careful, you might say yes to things that look good on the surface but don't align with your deeper purpose.

Emotional, mental, or physical obstacles (like stress, overwhelm, or lack of clarity) can drain your energy. When you're depleted, it's harder to stay intentional and grounded.

Internal obstacles like limiting beliefs, imposter syndrome, perfectionism, or fear of failure can cause you to unconsciously sabotage your progress—even when you're on the right path.

Life is full of competing priorities. The strategies in this final section will help you filter out noise and stay aligned with what truly matters. They act as a compass, keeping you on track even when things get chaotic.

With strategies in place, you're better prepared to handle those setbacks. You know your priorities, have backup plans, and can pivot without losing sight of your ultimate goal.

Peggi Cooney and Brigitta Dau

Chapter Ten

Imposter Syndrome

"You are not an imposter. You are a learner. And learners are allowed not to know everything."
-Dr. Valerie Young

Meditation

4 – 7 – 8 Breathing/Dr. Andrew Weil

Take a deep breath. Either sitting or standing, plant your feet firmly on the ground. Take several deep breaths, paying attention to your inhales and exhales.

Next, INHALE through your nose to the count of 4.

HOLD it for the count of 7.

EXHALE slowly through the mouth for the count of 8.

Repeat this pattern 3 more time.

Gnora wants your attention! Psst...If you think you're a fraud, you're probably not! Real frauds don't worry about being frauds. Imposter syndrome is just your brain's weird way of saying you care about doing well.

Imposter Syndrome Defined

What is imposter syndrome, and what does it have to do with achieving your goals? Reaching your North Star? Imposter syndrome and your North Star are deeply connected because imposter syndrome can cloud your vision, distort your sense of worth, and even lead you to chase a North Star that isn't truly yours.

Dr. Pauline Clance and Dr. Suzanne Imes first coined the term "imposter syndrome" when they published The Imposter Phenomenon in High Achieving Women: Dynamics and Therapeutic Intervention in 1978.

Imposter syndrome is a psychological pattern where high-achieving individuals doubt their accomplishments and fear being exposed as frauds, despite evidence of their success. It's characterized by persistent self-doubt and a fear of being discovered as incompetent, even when they have achieved significant results. This feeling can be debilitating, leading to anxiety, depression, and a reluctance to take on new challenges. If we don't take on new challenges, we do not have a chance of reaching our North Star.

Those of us who are high-achievers or overachievers often experience imposter syndrome. People with imposter syndrome doubt their abilities no matter what they've achieved. They often feel they don't deserve their accomplishments.

In addition, people who have imposter syndrome often identify as perfectionists. Imposter syndrome and perfectionism are closely related psychological experiences, often feeding into each other. Imposter syndrome involves feeling like a fraud despite evidence of competence, while perfectionism involves setting unrealistically high standards and being highly self-critical. This combination can lead to a cycle of overworking, anxiety, and low self-esteem. Perfectionism brings on heightened concern over making mistakes and a need for approval.

Perfectionism is driven primarily by internal pressures, such as the desire to avoid failure or harsh judgment. There is likely a social component as well, because perfectionistic tendencies have increased substantially among young people over the past 30 years, regardless of gender or culture.

Peggi: I can honestly say that I have never identified as a perfectionist, but I was a certified imposter syndrome sufferer. In 2018, I was awarded a UC Davis Continuing & Professional Education—Human Services Outstanding Service Award. I had only been teaching for four years. I felt like the biggest fraud on the planet. I thought, "There are so many other instructors that deserve this more. The two other instructors who received this award with me were my mentors. I couldn't possibly be on their level." Looking back at that time, my drinking had become problematic, and I thought if they only knew what was going on in my life, they would never have considered giving me this honor. Seven years into sobriety, and with all the work I have done on myself, I accept the award whole-heartedly.

Brigitta: I remember the first time I taught a mixed media art collage class. I felt like a total fraud. I'd never been to art school, and I think I took maybe one art class in high school. Yet there I was, standing in front of a group of women - getting paid - to guide them in creating their "manifestation pages" in their art journals. Now, after years of teaching similar classes, I see how unique each person's journey truly is. You don't need a degree in art to be creative, to express yourself, or to share your passion for personal growth.

The following are characteristics of having imposter syndrome. Do you see yourself in any of them?

- **Persistent Self-Doubt:**
  Individuals with imposter syndrome struggle to internalize their successes and often attribute them to luck, timing, or external factors rather than their own skills and hard work.
- **Fear of Exposure:**
  They constantly worry that others will realize they are not as competent as they appear, and they fear being exposed as a fraud.
- **Not a Mental Illness:**
  It's not a clinical diagnosis but rather a psychological pattern that can affect anyone, particularly common among high achievers.
- **Common Among High Achievers:**
  Studies show that a significant percentage of successful individuals experience imposter syndrome at some point in their lives.
- **Can be Relentless:**
  Even when presented with evidence of their competence, such as degrees, awards, or promotions, individuals with imposter syndrome may downplay or dismiss these achievements.

Impact of Imposter Syndrome:

- **Hindered Performance**:
  The fear of failure can lead to procrastination, perfectionism, and a reluctance to take on new challenges.
- **Emotional Distress:**
  Individuals with imposter syndrome may experience anxiety, depression, and low self-esteem.
- **Strained Relationships:**
  It can affect personal and professional relationships, as individuals may struggle to accept praise or build genuine connections.
- **Limited Career Growth:**
  The fear of being exposed can prevent individuals from pursuing promotions or taking on leadership roles.

Strategies we can use to overcome Imposter Syndrome:

- **Acknowledge and Validate Feelings:**
  Recognize that imposter syndrome is a common experience and that your feelings are valid, even if they are not based on reality.
- **Challenge Negative Thoughts:**
  Actively challenge the negative thoughts and beliefs that contribute to imposter syndrome. Replace them with more positive and realistic ones.
- **Focus on Accomplishments:**
  Keep a record of your accomplishments, both big and small, to remind yourself of your successes and build confidence.
- **Seek Support:**
  Talk to a therapist, counselor, or trusted friend or family member about your experiences.
- **Redefine Success:**
  Consider what success means to you personally and focus on internal measures of success rather than external validation.
- **Embrace Imperfection:**
  Accept that it's okay not to be perfect, and that everyone makes mistakes.
- **Don't Compare Yourself to Others:**
  Focus on your own journey and progress, rather than comparing yourself to others.
- **Celebrate Your Strengths:**
  Identify and celebrate your strengths and talents.

By understanding imposter syndrome and actively working to address it, you will be able to overcome the negative impact it has on your life and achieve your full potential. Doing the activities in this book can mitigate any thoughts of imposter syndrome you may be carrying.

Activity 1: A Simple Assessment Tool[18]

Borrowed from:
https://impostersyndrome.com.au/index.php/questionnaires/

1. You feel that you have fooled people in some way or have given the impression that you are more capable than you really are.
Very rarely = 1 *Sometimes = 2* *Almost always = 3*

2. You feel that your achievements are mainly down to good luck, other people's help or that the achievements weren't that big of a deal anyway.
Very rarely = 1 *Sometimes = 2* *Almost always = 3*

3. You find it hard to understand or accept how someone like you could be in the position you are in or be doing what you are doing.
Very rarely = 1 *Sometimes = 2* *Almost always = 3*

4. When you achieve something — for example, a qualification, a good result on a test, or a job promotion — you feel that there must have been some sort of mistake, maybe a clerical error or a computer error.
Very rarely = 1 *Sometimes = 2* *Almost always = 3*

5. When you make a mistake or something goes wrong, you feel worried that this could expose you as a fraud or prove that you don't know what you are doing.
Very rarely = 1 *Sometimes = 2* *Almost always = 3*

6. Despite your achievements, you feel that at any moment someone will come along and tap you on the shoulder and say, "We need to have a chat. You don't belong here."
Very rarely = 1 *Sometimes = 2* *Almost always = 3*

7. You find that each new success or achievement, instead of being a source of satisfaction, just increases the pressure to achieve the next time.
Very rarely = 1 *Sometimes = 2* *Almost always = 3*

Add up the total ____________.

So how did you score?

1-7: That's pretty unusual, but good for you.
This indicates that you rarely doubt your achievements and don't spend a lot of time wondering whether or not you are a fraud. In fact, you're probably surprised to hear that some people do question their abilities and doubt their achievements.

8-14: Most people will fall in this range.
Most of us will experience some imposter feelings from time to time, perhaps in a new situation or when we are going to be evaluated. The more often you experience them, the more likely they are to impact your life.

15-21: You frequently question your abilities and achievements and often feel like a fraud.
Imposter feelings are causing you some worry and probably having an impact on what you think, feel and do. This can have quite a limiting effect on your life.

Activity 2:
Journal Your Feelings About Your Assessment Results.

Chapter Eleven

Establishing a Routine
Are You a Morning or Night Person or a Little Bit of Both?

"Your future self drives your present actions."
-Dan Sullivan and Dr. Benjamin Hardy

Meditation: Single-Task Focus. (Let's all take a break from multitasking for a moment.)

Pick an activity, ANYTHING, and just give it your full attention for 3 minutes or more.

Examples:

- Sip your coffee without checking your email—become fully present and JUST sip your coffee.
- Turn off the radio (and phone) in your car and JUST drive.
- Take a walk without any devices.
- Take a bubble bath.
- Sit in your yard or a park.
- Listen to a meditation on the Insight Timer App.

If you are a morning person...

Morning routines help keep you tied to your purpose because they create intentional structure around your day, reinforcing your values, goals, and identity. They anchor you to your "why." A purposeful morning routine often includes activities like journaling, meditation, reading, or goal-setting. These practices help you reconnect with your deeper motivations and long-term vision before the distractions of the day begin.

Your first actions of the day shape your mental state. A purposeful routine helps you start the day with clarity, confidence, and focus—rather than stress or distraction. Self-care is often the first thing to go when you're rushing to get out the door in the morning. However, this principle is essential to your well-being. Find time to address your spiritual, physical and mental health. As soon as you wake up, take a few moments to meditate or pray. Take time to eat a satisfying breakfast. Give yourself a few moments of quiet time and perhaps review what you'd like to accomplish that day.

Once you've established your routine, simply keep it up. Doing these things day after day each morning will quickly turn into a habit. Once that occurs, you can go on autopilot, easily enjoying these healthy activities. Eventually, you may find that you have time to incorporate new positive habits into your morning routine.

Additionally, having a morning routine reduces decision fatigue; you waste less energy on trivial choices. You are less stressed. That frees up mental space for what really matters—your mission, your creativity, your purpose. And, you are less likely to forget something important.

It's crucial to let the people in your life know about your routine and how important it is to you. If you have guests in your home, or if you are visiting others, you need to let them know about your routine.

You don't need to cram everything into the early hours of your day. You can set your morning up for success by doing some tasks before you go to bed. That could mean hard-boiling a bunch of eggs or laying out what you want to wear. Figure out some things you can get done the night before to optimize your time in the morning.

Peggi: I need routine. I crave routine. I discovered this very early in my alcohol-free journey. Those first few minutes and hours after I wake up set the tone for my entire day. I get up at 4:30am. I need to be alone to do my journaling, writing, preparing for class if I am teaching that day, attending or facilitating a meeting, and savor a cup or two of my favorite coffee—Kona Island Sunrise with frothed milk and Not Pods toasted marshmallow almond and cocomut creamer (yes, heavenly). I exchange a gratitude list with my dear friend, Ann. I try to walk in the morning, weather permitting. I go over my "to do" list for the day and check my daily planner. My husband, family and friends all know my morning routine and honor it. Even my granddaughter Sawyer knows my morning routine when she spends the night.

Activity 1: Personalize Your Morning Routine/Journal Writing

Start by asking yourself what you want to accomplish before you leave the house. Do you want time to drink your coffee in peace before the kids wake up? Do you want to focus on your hair and makeup? Will a short workout help you feel better?

Figure out what's important to you and write it down. Then, plot out a tentative timetable so that you know how long you'll need to fit these priorities into your morning. This should give you a good idea of when you should set your alarm each morning.

Gnora explains that routines aren't boring—they're freedom! When the basics are on autopilot, you have more energy for the adventures and dreams that matter most.

So, what if you're not a morning person?

Do you have an evening routine instead? It can help you create a less hectic morning. It can also open the door for some magic in your life. With a nightly routine, you will utilize those last few minutes before going to sleep. You will be intentional with how you review your day and how you plan for tomorrow.

Start your evening by reviewing your wins. Write down anything worthy of personal praise. These can be big steps towards your North Star Goals and/or little steps towards maintaining your current trajectory.

Just doing this one activity nightly helps train your brain to manifest your desires. This, in turn, supports creating more momentum. You can also utilize this time to schedule tomorrow's wins. That's right. Schedule what could happen:

- What could be a win for tomorrow?
- What would you love to see happen tomorrow?

Don't get hung up on the details. Let your subconscious take care of that. Simply and clearly state what you WANT to see happen tomorrow.

In addition, you could spend a little time planning and scheduling the following day. If you know mornings are hectic for you, take a few minutes to jot down a few reminders before going to bed. By doing this, you can "hit the ground running" when the sun comes up. It's a concrete way to end the day and signals your brain that it is now time to rest.

Questions you could ask yourself: What will be my main goal for the day? What are the top three things I want to get done? Where will I choose to focus my attention? Where might I gain some ground in achieving my goals?

Supporting Yourself vs Brooding

What if you could use your sleep to problem solve? Planning the next day's contingency strategy before bedtime can be a huge support to your days. You can literally have your subconscious mind take on the problem-solving tasks that your conscious mind is too tired to handle.

Important note: Avoid brooding or ruminating on potential issues to come.

Some of us fall into the trap of obsessing over things when it's bedtime. Do not do that! The point of looking ahead to see what tomorrow may look like is to give yourself permission to sleep. You are choosing not to worry about these things. You are instead utilizing your subconscious to support you while you sleep.

If you know you simply can't go to bed without brooding about the issues, then leave this practice off of your nightly routine. Sleep is more important. Skip this activity if you know it will keep you awake or cause more anxiety before bedtime.

However, if you can be disciplined with yourself and allow your subconscious to do the work, reviewing upcoming challenges can sometimes prove to be helpful when used in a strategic evening routine.

Brigitta's example: Recently, I was prepping to teach various crafts at an art retreat in San Diego. One of the skills they asked me to teach was cross-stitch. This is a craft I know of and admire but, up until now, hadn't done it myself. I was given several weeks not just to learn this skill, but to teach it! I knew using my subconscious mind would be the fastest way to prepare for this retreat. And so, my first step was to review a few cross-stitch videos before going to bed. Then, the next day when I sat down to learn and teach this craft, it didn't feel so foreign to me. In fact, I felt confident about it, and I picked it up quickly. Why? Because I used my subconscious to learn this new skill.

Peggi's example: Although I am very much a morning person, my nighttime routine is also very important to me. At about 8:30 pm, I begin to get ready for bed. I straighten my desk, put out anything I need for the next day. I listen to Yoga Nidra on the free meditation app, Insight Timer. Jennifer Piercy is my favorite. I rarely hear the end of the meditations that last from 15 to 30 minutes. Sometimes I wake up with various thoughts that keep me from going back to sleep. I keep a notepad and pen next to my bed so that I can write the thoughts down, getting them out of my brain so that I can settle back to sleep. So, I guess you could say I'm both a morning and a night person.

Activity 2: Night-time Journal / Day Timer Prompts

- List your wins from today.
- List your desired wins for tomorrow.
- Schedule tomorrow so you can "hit the ground running" and signal your brain it's time to sleep.
- List future potential issues for your subconscious to solve while you sleep. (SKIP THIS if you know this will lead to anxiety and keep you awake.)

Chapter Twelve

Change Your Energy, Change Your Life

"Your personality creates your personal reality. Your personality is made up of how you act, how you think and how you feel. Our life begins to change when we change our energy."
--Dr. Joe Dispenza

Meditation: Alternate Nostril Breathing/Ancient Yoga Tradition

- Sit comfortably and take three breaths.
- Using your fingers of your dominant hand, close your right nostril.
- Inhale through your left nostril.
- Close your left nostril, open your right nostril and exhale through your right nostril.
- Next, inhale through your right nostril. Then close it and exhale through your left nostril.
- Repeat this breathing, inhaling and exhaling through alternate nostrils for three to five breaths.
- Return to breathing normally.

Use the Think, Feel, Act Cycle to Create Positive Energy

This is not a chapter about "woo woo", not that we don't love us some "woo woo" on occasion.

Truth bomb: Your habitual daily mindset will absolutely affect your energy. And depending on the quality of your energy, it will direct your life in either a positive or a negative way. Let's take a quick look at how our minds affect our energy and behaviors.

EVERY action that we take begins with a thought. This is how we're wired. We have an idea, then experience an emotion based on that thought. Those emotions are what motivate all of our behaviors. This is now known as the "Think, Feel, Act Cycle" created by Dr. Aaron T. Beck.[19]

Boiled down to basics:
We have a thought. (**Think**)
We experience an emotion based on that thought. **(Feel)**
We do something (or refuse to do it) based on the feelings generated by the thought. (**Act**)

From there we have more thoughts, more feelings and continue to act or refuse to act based on those thoughts and feelings. What has this got to do with energy?

Every emotion carries an energetic charge to it. You know this to be true. Compare a happy person to a depressed person and you cannot deny that when you are around them, their energies are wildly different. And we've all walked into a room where a loud argument has occurred and "felt" the energy in the room.

What about those moments when we meet someone and know immediately that something is not right? We call this our "gut feeling". We may not know why, but something about them is setting off warning bells in our bodies.

What about positive energy? Let's talk about "charismatic" people. "Charisma" is an interesting frequency because it has a powerful effect on us. Charismatic people are often artists, influencers, or leaders. They can seem to have an innate magical power within them. Usually, it's difficult to pinpoint exactly what it is about charismatic people that makes them so magnetic. It's not necessarily their appearance. It's something else. They seem to exude an undefinable energy that draws people to them like moths to light.

So, how is it that some people can set off alarm bells and others can seem enchanting without even uttering a word? Simple. Their energy.

So, how can we change our energy in a way that supports us as we journey towards our North Star? How can we shift out of lower energetic behaviors like procrastination and laziness? How can we instead become more motivated, enthusiastic, and magnetic? By utilizing our innate "think, feel, act cycle" to calibrate our energy.

Your thoughts and feelings automatically generate a specific energy. The more you think certain thoughts, the more of that particular energy you create. This can work for both positive and negative thoughts. Ruminating about something negative is nothing more than repeatedly thinking negative thoughts. The resulting low energy feelings continue to be generated until you break out of that cycle. The same can be true for higher energetic thoughts. Think inspiring thoughts on an endless loop, and pretty soon you'll be feeling inspired.

If you start thinking those inspired thoughts daily, they can become habitual. Once those thoughts are habitual, they become your new mindset. Before long, you will be exuding that energy on a daily basis.

Gnora is famous for saying. Don't be a Debbie Downer. Be like Vibrant Vivian!

This is NOT the practice of repeating positive affirmations to ourselves in front of the mirror. Yes, affirmations can be a somewhat helpful tool to replace our negative self-talk. However, if we want to create lasting change, they won't be truly effective. We want to live our lives in a way that pulls us in the direction of our goals and values. Creating a high energy mindset is the most effective way to do this.

The difference between a mindset and an affirmation is best explained by reworking this well-known phrase: "When one door closes, another door opens." This sounds positive but is ultimately a vague and unhelpful sentence. It also elicits no emotional charge at all. It's wishful thinking at best. But a person with a high energy, creative mindset would rewrite that phrase and establish a mantra that says, "When one door closes, look for a window and if there isn't one, knock the wall down."

These two sentences carry very different energetic frequencies, don't they? Read them again and decide which one is calibrated at a higher level of energy?

"When one door closes, another one opens".
"When one door closes, find a window and if there isn't one, knock down the wall."

Obviously, the second sentence feels more energizing and requires action on your part. And who would you rather be? The person hoping for a way out (positive affirmation) or the person creating their own pathway (creative mindset)? Which person's energy is more likely to lead to success?

Changing our energy can literally be this easy. However, this isn't a "one and done" thing either. This has to become a daily habit. To raise your energetic frequency, you have to be repeatedly thinking high-energy thoughts. And yes, changing your energy absolutely changes your life.

Activity 1: Notice Your Thoughts

For three days, stop what you're doing and notice what you are thinking several times throughout the day. We recommend scheduling these timeouts into your day or setting an alarm. Just stop and notice.

- What am I thinking?
- What am I feeling?
- Am I taking action or avoiding doing something?
- How does my energy feel?

Then, decide if you would like to change your energy. If yes, choose different thoughts and notice if they elicit the feelings you want to feel. How does your energy feel now?

Activity 2: Journaling Your Thoughts

In your journal, write out a list of feelings you would like to experience on a daily basis.

- What sort of mindset would you like to create for yourself?
- What thoughts and feelings would you need to cultivate to create that mindset?
- What would you feel energetically if you were totally aligned with those thoughts and feelings?

Write out your new thoughts and post them anywhere that you might need a reminder. Practice replacing your old thoughts with these new thoughts every time you catch yourself lapsing back into your old habitual thinking.

Brigitta's example of changing her mindset: Becoming a Non-Smoker

In my early 20s I was a daily smoker. I won't lie; I loved smoking. I also knew I had to quit if I wanted to achieve my goals and live a healthy life in the process. But I was 100% addicted to nicotine. So, how did I get through those first few weeks? (By the way, this was in the late 80's so tools like "the patch" and "Nicorette" did not yet exist.) I changed my mindset and put it on an endless repeat loop in my head. I decided how I wanted to feel and how I would behave, and I created a new thought that would encapsulate it all:

I AM A "NON-SMOKER".

That was my number one thought. The moment I woke up craving my first cigarette of the day, I said out loud, "I am a NON-SMOKER." If I caught myself fantasizing about smoking, I'd stop and repeat this thought over and over in my head. I followed this thought with the actions of what I imagined a healthy person would do, such as drink a lot of water. Sometimes I'd go for a run. Sometimes I'd simply distract myself with something to keep my mind off cigarettes. Whatever I did, I did it with the energy and conviction of a NON-SMOKER. I thought it, felt it, acted on it, and aligned my energy to this new reality.

I went from being a two-pack a day smoker to a total non-smoker. It was one of the hardest things I've ever done in my life. What's even more amazing is that I quit the first time I tried. Why? Because I changed my mindset and my energy.

Peggi's example of changing her mindset:

When my current employer asked me if I wanted to be a social work instructor, I jumped at the chance. And then I had second thoughts, because I knew I would have to put on a training demonstration to staff to get the position. I almost didn't go through with it because I had applied to teach for the University of Phoenix and had to put on a similar demonstration, and I didn't get hired.

I shared my worries with my soul coach at the time, and she said I needed to change the way I approached this task. Sherrie Ataide, (owner of Life Design in Chico, California) said, "They are not interviewing you. You are interviewing them. Ask yourself if they are the right fit for you, not the other way around." I followed her advice, did well on my presentation, and I got my dream job. Sherrie's advice has applied to many other aspects of my life, around therapy, friendships, memberships, and organizations.

Chapter Thirteen

Crazy Makers and Energy Vampires

"Crazy-makers keep you off balance, derail your time, and rob you of your confidence."
—Julia Cameron

Meditation: Buckets of Gold

This is a lovely practice to neutralize lingering negative thoughts. Sometimes, even if a conflict has been resolved, our unhelpful thoughts continue to loop. This practice helps clear that energy.

Close your eyes. Think of the situation that is causing negative thoughts. Visualize or imagine this issue right in front of you.

Now imagine there is a huge bucket floating above this image. Notice the bucket tipping and visualize a stream of gold light pouring down onto the negative situation. Watch the experience become totally drenched in this effervescent, golden light.

Continue to visualize this bucket of gold endlessly drenching this image…until you feel your negative thoughts dissipate.

Repeat this meditation as needed.

Crazy Makers

We cannot encourage you to travel towards your North Star without addressing some obstacles that will come up. The biggest one is other people. Julia Cameron talks a great deal about "Crazy Makers" in her book, The Artist's Way.

What exactly is a crazy-maker? Julia Cameron writes this: "Crazy-makers are those personalities that create storm centers. They are often charismatic, frequently charming, highly inventive, and powerfully persuasive. They can also be enormously destructive. They break deals and destroy schedules, expect special treatment, spend your time and money, and blame you when things go wrong. They are expert blamers. They are the kind of people who can take over your whole life if you let them."[20]

Does this sound like anyone you know? If yes, then let's talk about how to manage these people.

Step One is to discern your priorities. Where do you truly want to spend your time and energy, and with whom? Your North Star goals should sit at the very top of this priority list. Be sure to include all of your self-care practices here too. These aren't indulgences. They are essentials. Non-negotiables. You can also add hobbies as priorities to be prioritized in terms of time, money and energy.

Step Two: set strong boundaries. The word boundaries can stir up a lot of feelings. How do you feel about setting them? Does it make you uncomfortable? Do you worry that having clear boundaries will make you less likable? Does the word itself bring up resistance or guilt?

Many of us were never taught how to set healthy boundaries. The good news: it's a skill you can learn. Boundaries aren't an inborn trait that only a few people have. Everyone can learn how to set effective boundaries.

When you say no to things that don't align with your North Star, you're:

- Preserving energy for what truly matters.
- Avoiding distractions that pull you off course.
- Creating space for intentional choices that reflect your deeper purpose.

Once you've identified where boundaries are needed, enforce them consistently. Say no to the hysterical coffee talks and let the frantic texts go unanswered. Tired of book clubs where no one talks about the book? Your time and energy are valuable, limited resources. Guard them wisely!

Saying no is saying YES to your North Star. Every "no" is actually a "yes" to something else. Saying no to over-committing is saying yes to well-being. Saying no to busywork is saying yes to meaningful impact. Saying no to people-pleasing is saying yes to authenticity.

Your boundaries are not barriers- they're the framework that protects your North Star. And they are essential when dealing with crazy makers.

Energy Vampires

Energy vampires—those who consistently drain your emotional, mental, or even physical energy—are especially detrimental when you're fueling your North Star. They hijack your emotional bandwidth. They can be chronically negative people, manipulators, or drama creators. They can demand your time but offer little value or reciprocity. They disregard your boundaries.

These people take crazy-making to a new level. They may or may not be friends or family members. The influence that these people have can be both impressive and damaging. You will know when you have been drained by an energy vampire when you experience one or both of these things:

1. You will feel like you have taken a major sedative after being around them, or you have been holding your breath.
2. You will feel like you literally need to "shake them off" and might actually find yourself shaking or pacing about.

Belinda Davidson, spiritual teacher and medical intuitive, writes.

> "Energy vampires are those who, knowingly or unknowingly, plug into your energy field and draw from it - especially if your boundaries are weak. They leave your feeling exhausted, confused, and off-track from your soul path."[21]

Your North Star requires clarity, energy, and focus. Energy vampires disrupt all three. They can cloud your thinking, distort your thoughts, derail your actions, and may make you doubt your path or lose sight of your goals.

Protect your energy, and you protect your purpose. Saying no to energy vampires isn't selfish—it's strategic. It's how you stay emotionally available for what matters. It keeps your thoughts focused on your vision. It's how you take action that builds your legacy, not someone else's drama.

Gnorth reminds us that "No" is a complete sentence!

Brigitta's personal example (Only one??? Y'all, I live in LA...it's the homeland of crazy-makers and energy vampires!)

I was speaking with a potential coaching client. This woman and I were discussing the possibility of my working as a life coach with her son.

My alarm bells were going off within the first few seconds of this call. The first red flag was her telling me she "loved me" and that having me work with her son was "going to be amazing!". She had not checked out my website or done any research into me at all. She was basing this opinion on the person who had referred me to her and our thirty-second conversation. My "spidey senses" were activated.

Within about five minutes, our conversation had shifted into an entirely new tone. This time she was exclaiming confusion over the fact that I was "unwilling to be available for her 24/7" and she was feeling "unheard" in our conversation exchange. That's quite an about-face from gushing with her overflow of love.

The speed at which she spiraled was mainly due to my not giving an inch. Energy vampires get frantic and out of control when they are shut down so quickly. To be blunt, they are used to getting their way because they are insidious and resourceful in finding your weak spots. Because I am an energy practitioner as well as a life coach, I can spot this fairly quickly. Unfortunately for her, she experienced a fast and furious meltdown due to slamming directly into my ironclad boundaries.

We managed to end the call politely.

And the second I hung up, I literally ran around shaking off my arms to discharge her energy. I had been exposed to an energy vampire.

We did not work together. And I felt sorry for her son, who probably really could have used some stable support.

Peggi's personal example:

I worked for a manager who I let make me feel less than. She would constantly put me down, especially in front of other people. In fact, it was so noticeable, one of my colleagues who worked in another department asked me, "Why do you let her treat you like that?" I was so embarrassed that I answered, "She's just kidding." Inside, I knew the truth, but I felt shame for letting her treat me that way. She made fun of how many times I was married, how random my comments were, how after I got my MSW I was one of "those people" and she even said in front of one of my staff, "I can make Peggi cry whenever I want."

This manager was nothing short of a bully. It took me years to finally stand up for myself, and shortly after, I made a two-year plan to retire.

Activity 1: Energy Drains

Take an inventory of your friends, family, colleagues, etc.
Can you identify any crazy-makers or energy vampires in your life?
If yes, journal about the ways they are creating drama and draining your energy.
Brainstorm solutions:

- What boundaries can you set?
- How can you implement them?
- Can you prepare and plan ahead for when they try to challenge your boundaries? (Which they will…) Or,
- Do you need to remove them from your life altogether?

Activity 2: Choose ANY Meditation and Practice Daily

Activity 3: Permission Slip to Say "No":

I, ____, am granted FULL permission to whole heartedly say NO to _______________________, _______________________________, & ________________________________.

________________ ____

Date Signature

Chapter Fourteen

Self-Mapping Using the Three Questions and Solution-Focused Inquiry

"What you water, grows."
author unknown

Meditation: Pick a Color

Just like the game we used to play on long car trips, choose a color and notice all the places you see it.

Just for today, notice this color. When you see it, stop what you are doing and simply notice it. Or, go one step further and notice how noticing that color makes you feel?

Then tomorrow, pick another color.

Building the Foundation to Self-Mapping:

Three Simple Questions

Peggi's career in social work introduced her to a practice called "Safety Organized Practice". At the foundation of this practice are three simple questions:

- What is working well?
- What am I worried about?
- What needs to happen next?

Once we have determined what our North Star is, the next thing we need to do is assess where we are in the process. Then, we want to revisit it at intervals of our choosing. I mapped my progress in becoming alcohol-free. In the beginning, I mapped my first 30 days of being alcohol-free, then 60 days, 90 days, and now I map at the beginning of every year to assess the highlights, barriers of the previous year and plan for the new year.

What is working well?

What are some of the things you can list that are working well in relation to reaching your goals/North Star? These are your strengths. Think in terms of actual examples. No "working well" is too small. In other words, if I were a fly on the wall, what would I see you doing? For example, if your goal is to eat unprocessed food, some working-wells could be that you tossed all the processed food in your kitchen; you signed up for Hungry Root delivery; you joined a support group, or you commit to not eating any food with more than five preservatives or artificial additives.

Here are some areas of strength:

- Formal and informal supports
- Spirituality
- Self-esteem
- Self-efficacy
- Emotional regulation
- Problem solving
- Communication skills to express our needs and ideas

What am I worried about?

In order to create a balanced assessment of where you are right now in terms of moving closer to your goals, it is important to look at the worries you currently have and address the barriers and obstacles you may encounter along the way. We introduced obstacles in Chapter Five of the WOOP model. Ask yourself: What's going to get in the way of the result that you want? These will turn into next steps.

What needs to happen next?

Do you need to change or update anything? Do you need to plan for obstacles and barriers? These will be your next steps to reach the goals you set for yourself. Next steps should be SMART Goals: Specific, Measurable, Achievable, Relative, and Time-Limited. This method ensures that your goals are clear, realistic, and time-bound, enhancing your chances of success. You can use the SMART Goal method for any type of goal setting, personally and professionally.

- **Specific**: A specific goal clearly defines what you want to accomplish. It answers questions like: What do I want to achieve? Why is this goal important? Who is involved?
- **Measurable**: Measurable goals allow you to track your progress and determine when you've achieved your objective. This involves quantifying your goal with metrics or data points.
- **Achievable**: An achievable goal is realistic and attainable within your current re sources and constraints. It should challenge you; it should sit right outside your comfort zone, where optimal learning takes place.
- **Relevant**: A relevant goal aligns with your broader objectives and values. It ensures that the goal matters to you and is worthwhile. You must have an emotional attachment to the goal. Make sure it's your goal, not someone else's.
- **Time-bound**: Time-bound goals have a clear deadline or timeframe, creating a sense of urgency and prompting action.

Here is a SMART Goal Example for writing this book:

- **Specific:** Brigitta and Peggi will write a book titled Finding Your North Star: A Guide to Finding Your Life's Purpose.
- **Measurable:** It should be at least 30,000 words long, and they want to spend at least six hours per week working on it.
- **Attainable:** They are both published writers, love the subject, have the time, and work well together.
- **Relevant:** Brigitta and Peggi have vast experience in the subject through teaching, coaching, lived experience, acting (Brigitta), social work (Peggi), and feel that they would like to expand their knowledge to a much broader audience.
- **Time-bound:** We plan to finish the first draft by October 31, 2025.

Solution Focused Inquiry:

Solution-focused inquiry (SFQ's) reflect the basic belief that problems are best solved by focusing on what is already working, and how a client would like their life to be, rather than focusing on the past and the origin of problems. Using solution-focused questions can help you with the mapping process.

Developed by Steven DeShazer and Insoo Kim Berg in the 1980s and 1990s, solution-focused questions are a shift away from just looking at problems to a search for what's worked in the past. Problems are best solved by focusing on what is already working, and how a person would like their life to be.

SFQ's can be a huge help for people moving out of the problem and into their own best solution. They take very little time to do. And most importantly, SFQ's help us take ownership and therefore make us active players in our behavior change.

There are five types of solution-focused questions and examples:

Exception Questions: Has there ever been a time [the problem] could have happened... maybe almost did...but somehow you were able to do something different?

- Was there a time before in your life when you were able to accomplish this or a similar goal? What did that look like? What strategies did you utilize?
- Describe a time you successfully stepped outside your comfort zone. What enabled you to get through?
- Who/what supports did/do you use to move you closer to your goals?

Scaling Questions: On a scale of one to ten (I don't start at 0—no one is a zero) with 1 being the least of something (like your South Star) and 10 being the most (like your North Star), what would your number be?

Follow-up questions:
What made you pick that number?
What do you think would need to happen to increase your rating by one?

You can scale willingness, confidence, capacity and progress.

Gnorth is not a fan of math and numbers. He reminds us: The numbers on the scale have no real meaning—they help you put your strengths and worries into words.

Relationship or Position Questions: Questions designed to help someone shift perspective and see through another's eyes?

- What would someone close to you say your strengths or weaknesses are?
- What would your significant other or children think about the goal you have set for yourself?

Coping and Preferred Future Questions:

- The things you have been going through are not easy. How do you think you have been able to do as well as you have so far?
- You are pretty clear that this is not how you want things to be. How would you like things to be instead? What needs to happen for things to be like that?
- What do you see yourself doing in one, three or five years?

Activity 1: Complete Your North Star Map

We have provided a sample of mapping for you to use as a guide. This is an adaptation of Sue Lohrbach's Consultation and Information Framework.[22] Using the blank mapping form and SFQ's, fill out your first map.

Don't forget to schedule your next mapping. This can be done at intervals of your choosing. Recommended intervals are 30, 60, 90 days, six months, nine months, one year.

North Star Self-Mapping Example

Purpose for Mapping: *Current Status for Writing Finding Your North Star*
Date: 11/15/2025

What is working well?	What am I worried about? What are the current barriers?	What needs to happen next? (who, what, when?) Make your goals SMART
• Our core values are aligned; we work so well together; we have a good system • Our book just came back from our editor, Val and we made the suggested changes (she loves the book!) • Stacy has agreed to design our book cover • Met with our publisher, Robin/Leaning Rock Press • We have eight beta readers	• Time: we both have other careers, interests and commitments that can get in the way • We haven't had much time to think about book promotion and social media	• Over the next 90 days, Brigitta and I will meet weekly, working with our team to meet our March 2026 publish deadline • Get feedback from our beta readers • Create a Facebook and Instagram page • Start collecting e-mails for those interested in reading our book

Next Mapping Date: 1/15/2026

North Star Self-Mapping

Purpose for Mapping:
Date:

What is working well?	What am I worried about? What are the current barriers?	What needs to happen next? (who, what, when?) Make your goals SMART

Next mapping Date: ______________________________

After you complte your map, answer the following:

- What are you feeling after completing your map?
- Were there any surprises? Write those in your notes.

Subsequent Mapping

It is important to track your progress. Your first map serves as a baseline. Subsequent mapping tells you if the tools and strategies you are using are moving you closer to your North Star or if you may need to make some upgrades. It's great to revisit your mapping at intervals like 90 days, six months, 12 months, etc.

- How does your map look now?
- Which column is longer-wells or worries? ("wells" should be longer and worries shorter at this point.)
- Do you need to change any next steps?

Chapter Fifteen

Managing Fear and Overwhelm

"It's not my thoughts about worthlessness that were the problem. The problem was that I took myself to be them."
— Geneen Roth.

Meditation: Present Moment Sound Bath

Either sitting or standing, close your eyes and take 3 deep breaths.

Notice any sounds around you. Next, notice the FURTHEST sound you can hear. Settle on this sound and ponder it for several breaths.

Next, notice the CLOSEST sound you can hear. Settle on this sound and ponder it for several breaths.

Next, notice a sound somewhere between these two sounds. Settle on this one for several breaths.

Do you have a sound you prefer?

Getting to the Bottom of Your Fear and Overwhelm

Psychology is now moving towards a more holistic approach when dealing with our critical self-talk and the wild array of emotions it creates. "Internal Family Systems" (IFS) was founded by Dr. Richard C. Schwartz and is commonly utilized by psychologists, therapists, coaches, and counselors. Dr. Schwartz began his now evidence-based treatment over a decade ago when traditional therapy was failing his patients. He first utilized his approach with his patients battling eating disorders and soon sought to have it included as a tool for all forms of therapy. It is now a widely used technique for all walks of life, from extreme PTSD cases to people wishing to create lasting change in their lives.

Dr. Swartz explains;

> The goal of IFS is to embody the Self (our "essence") and heal our injured parts (uncomfortable emotional activations) so that we can live with confidence, guided by curiosity and compassion. When people embody more of their Self and listen to their parts rather than trying to eliminate these aspects of themselves, their inner dialogues change spontaneously. Their extreme voices calm down, and they begin to feel good things: safer, lighter, freer, more open, more playful.[23]

This approach asks us to listen to our parts rather than to ignore them. In other words, allowing your feelings to have a voice and actually listening to your thoughts, vs avoiding them altogether. This mindset allows for a more compassionate and ultimately more respectful relationship with ourselves.

For our purposes, let's talk about those parts of ourselves that are triggered when we are feeling fear and overwhelm. Understanding fear and overwhelm through IFS is crucial for staying aligned with your North Star because these emotional states often signal the presence of protective parts that are trying to help but may unintentionally derail your path.

The important thing is to acknowledge that they are a part of us. We want to remember that when we are feeling overwhelmed, we are not overwhelm itself. Something has triggered us to *feel* overwhelmed. It can feel like this emotion has taken us over, but it is still only a part of us. This is an important and useful distinction.

These parts, "fear and overwhelm", are a specific representation of how we are feeling at the moment. And at their core, they are here to help us. Their job, as counterintuitive as it seems at times, is to keep us safe. For example, a more "helpful" reaction of fear being triggered is when a fire alarm goes off. At that time, you WANT adrenaline to rush through your limbs and your mind to be on high alert. However, you don't need that same level of adrenaline and energy when pitching your project ideas to a table full of people or asking someone out on a date. But unless you've created a healthy relationship with your fear, it will show up in full force (fire alarm energy!) every time it's triggered. This is why both fear and overwhelm can feel almost paralyzing at times. The level of intensity at which they are appearing is disproportionate to the event at hand.

"Feel the fear and do it anyway" is a somewhat outdated solution to managing our fear and overwhelm. It may work for some people, but it fails many of us. And here's why; it leaves out any option for growth and internal strength. It suggests we "white knuckle" our way through our anxiety. The willpower required for this approach is a huge drain on our energy and not a sustainable resource. Also, if we are only "powering through" we are likely exhausted. We are unlikely to cultivate any inner growth or improved self-esteem when we feel wiped out.

By engaging with our fears versus shutting them out, we are more likely to gain self-confidence and self-compassion. And these two qualities, unlike force and willpower, are limitless resources because they are restorative mindsets by nature.

So, how can we create a healthier relationship with our fear and overwhelm?

By talking with them.

Stick with us here.

- Notice fear and overwhelm as signals, not enemies.
- Listen to the parts behind them with compassion and curiosity.
- Unblend from those parts so your Self can lead.
- Reassure those parts that your North Star is safe and trustworthy.

This allows you to move forward with clarity, courage, and compassion—the qualities of Self that fuel your North Star. As we've been saying, these feelings are "parts" of who we are. If we can see our fear as a differentiated part of our Self, then we can communicate with it.

Let's be honest. If you are trying something new or embarking on a big goal, fear and overwhelm have a rightful seat on that journey. In fact, if you "weren't" afraid, we'd be afraid. So, your anxious parts are welcome participants on this expedition. The distinction to make is that they are not behind the steering wheel. YOU are at the helm.

Activity 1:
Create an open communication between you and your feelings.

This activity is inspired by IFS but is not a substitute for working with an IFS-trained therapist.

Close your eyes and imagine your fear sitting across from you. Take a moment to really look at it. Is it a younger version of you? Is it a big protector type of person? Does it resemble a parent or a teacher from your past? Trust whatever comes up.

Then, ask your **Fear:**

"What are you afraid of?" "What part of me is afraid right now, and what does it need to feel safe enough to let me lead?"

Let it tell you everything. Give it your full attention and be curious. Take your time, remain open, and hear what it's saying. Let it go off on any tangents it may have. This is a part of you wishing to be heard and acknowledged.

Listen to your fear.

Continue this conversation until it's feeling seen and heard. This might take only a few minutes or it might take fifteen minutes. (Also know that this will likely not be your only conversation with this part.). Then, thank your fear for sharing with you. Thank it for its time.

Write about your experience in your journal. Include noting if any of your fear's beliefs are actually true. Are they helpful? If so, make a note of that. Are some of these fearful thoughts based on an experience from childhood that is now no longer relevant? That's helpful information too. That means you have an opportunity to practice self-compassion with this wounded part of you.

Finally, examine how you can utilize all of this information.

Gnora adds: Talking to your fear isn't crazy—ignoring it is! Fear usually has something important to tell you, even if it's just 'Hey, this matters to you!' Listen with curiosity, not judgment.

Next, have a conversation with your **Overwhelm.** Listen and acknowledge its feelings and try to understand why it feels that way.

After completing this activity, you will have a much more honest relationship with these parts of yourself. You can converse with any of your emotional parts as much as you want to. The goal is to include all of your parts without being hijacked by any of them.

Brigitta's personal example:

My first experience of doing this "parts work" was years ago when I was teaching Pilates at an exclusive gym in Los Angeles. An incident occurred that threw me into the middle of a conflict between a few "popular" gym members and management. I was very upset! All I wanted to do was shut down, hit the eject button, and numb out all at once. At that time, my "go to" numbing behavior involved binging on huge amounts of carbs and sugar. What I really wanted to do was go straight to a donut shop, buy a dozen donuts plus a dozen cookies and consume all of them on the drive home. The resulting sickness, not to mention self-loathing and shame, would have kept me depressed and exhausted for at least a day or two afterwards. I decided to give this new approach a try instead. Here is what I discovered.

Me: Hi. I'm here. I see you. Can we talk?

Fear: I'm scared. I hate this. I need to run away.

Me: I can see that. But I'm here. What can I do to help? What are you afraid of?

Fear: They don't like me. They are going to make fun of me. They are going to bully me again. I hate feeling like this. What's wrong with me? I'm a weirdo. People hate me. I can't do this. Don't make me stay here.

Me: Sweetheart, come here. Let me hold you. How old are you, honey?

Fear: Seven.

Me: No one is going to bully you. No one is going to make you do anything, okay? I'm right here. I won't let them hurt you. Tell me what else is going on.

Fear: I want to run away. I want to be alone. I can't do this.

Me: You don't have to handle this, honey. I'm in charge now. Look at me, I'm all grown up. And those people are not those mean girls. These are different people now. I've got this. You don't have to worry about them, I'm the grownup here. You get to be seven years old. You don't have to be a grownup. Let me give you a hug. How can I help you feel less afraid?

Fear: I don't know…

Me: What if we hold hands? And if we have to deal with them, I'll do all the talking. Okay? I've got this. What else can we do? Maybe you can bring Chipmunk with you ("Chipmunk" was my most beloved toy as a child).

Fear: (with a slight smile). Okay. I guess so.

Me: Nobody is going to bully you. I'm here now. They've got to get past me to get to you, and that's not going to happen. I promise. Thank you for sharing your feelings with me.

From this exchange, I was able to love my way through an old trigger and learn from my fear. This was also my first step to freedom from my self-destructive behaviors with food.
I also realized that despite years of traditional therapy, my wounds from being bullied as a child were not completely healed. I knew these feelings would continue to hold me back if they weren't addressed. By allowing this vulnerable part of me to express herself and be reassured, I could begin to create a relationship with my vulnerability. Now, I can sense when this insecurity is getting activated. I can feel her, acknowledge her, and take care of her as well as manage the situation at hand. She is no longer burdened with feeling like she has to be in charge. And because of this, I can now take risks in ways I never could have before. I'm not bypassing my fears. Instead, I'm moving forward with them, with Chipmunk in hand.

Activity 2: Carpooling With All of Your Parts

Close your eyes and imagine you are behind the steering wheel of a minivan. Before you drive away, you double-check the rear-view mirror. You see both fear and overwhelm buckled up safely in the back seat. Maybe they are anxiously fidgeting with their seatbelts. Now notice a third buddy buckled in between the two of them—enthusiasm. You laugh. Enthusiasm is offering to share their snacks with fear and overwhelm. Uh huh… those three have a LOT in common! And they are all along for the ride. Except for one important thing:
YOU are in the driver's seat.

(Note: if this activity resonates with you and you would like to dive deeper, please check out Dr. Schwartz's book found in our resource section.)

Chapter Sixteen

Catastrophic and All or Nothing Thinking

"Your worst-case scenario is rarely reality, It's just your fear playing dress-up."
-author unknown

Meditation: Labels can be a Good Thing

Take a look at your surroundings and label what you see. Be very specific in only naming these items versus getting caught up in the story behind them.

For example: water on the floor.
Rather than jumping to your thoughts about it, "Why is there water on the floor? Someone could slip and hurt themselves! I live with a household of slobs!" just label it: "water on floor"

Name at least 10 items. If you are still getting caught up in your thoughts about these items, continue naming and labeling items until you can observe them without opinions.

Catastrophic Thinking

Your North Star requires vision, courage, and trust. Catastrophic thinking replaces those with fear-based decision-making, avoidance of growth opportunities, or self-sabotage. Instead of moving toward your purpose, you start reacting to imagined threats.

Catastrophizing is a cognitive distortion that can shut us down before we even start. You know you are in the throes of catastrophic thinking when your mind leaps straight to the worst possible outcome. If you experience a small setback but view it as a massive failure, your thoughts are skewing catastrophic. If you dismiss any and all potential positive outcomes, that is also a sign that you are stuck in the catastrophizing mindset.

Because our brains are wired to avoid pain (this is how we've survived as long as we have), we will not take any actions that may lead to despair and/or failure. This particular "overthinking loop" breeds anxiety and can be triggered by high-stake situations, past traumas, and perfectionistic tendencies.

A quick example shows how paralyzing this thought distortion can be. Let's say you have a presentation to do. A certain amount of worry and anxiety would be expected for most of us. However, a person caught in catastrophic thinking would go to the worst-case scenario in their mind. Rather than thinking proactively and preparing diligently for the event, the person with the catastrophic mind would instead be thinking "If I mess this up everyone will think I'm an idiot, and I'll lose my job, and my life will fall apart…"

You can see how debilitating this thinking is.

But major experiences aren't the only things that can trigger this thought process. Catastrophic thinking can also be activated by something as simple as uncertainty.

What? Yes. This puts us in a bit of a conundrum, doesn't it? If you are setting your sights on your North Star, you will likely be stepping out of your comfort zone. In other words, you will be expected to take action in the face of uncertainty.

How can we override our brain's desire to catastrophize? Here are four tools to try when dealing with this thinking loop.

- Do a reality check. What is actually happening and what realistically could go wrong?
- Rate this situation on a scale from 1-10 with 1 being nothing to worry about and 10 being a full-blown disaster. (Most of our situations, even the really stressful ones, usually come in around a 3 or 4.)
- Interrupt your thinking by taking a time out and doing one of the meditations in this book.
- Respond to your "doomsday" self-talk with the opposite. "What could go right?"

Gnorth points out: Both Faith and Fear require you to believe in someting you cannot see. Which do you choose?

All-or-Nothing Thinking

All-or-nothing thinking, also known as black-and-white thinking can significantly distort how you relate to your North Star. We see this cognitive distortion as the "first cousin" to catastrophic thinking.

Where catastrophizing has us exaggerating the negative impact of an event, all-or-nothing thinking sees all options and outcomes in the extremes. There is no middle ground with all-or-nothing thinking. It's success vs failure, perfect vs worthless.

A healthier mindset is "progress over perfection." Instead of all-or-nothing. Try "both/and" or progressive thinking like:

- I didn't hit the mark today, but I am still on the path.
- This setback taught me something valuable.
- I can be proud of the effort even if the outcome isn't perfect.

(Looking back at The Goal Attainment Rating Scale GARS in Chapter Six.)

Catastrophic thinking leads to anxiety, whereas the all-or-nothing thinking results in feelings of shame and defeat. Both of these mindsets are paralyzing and erase any option for balance.

Activity 1: Write Down Your Thoughts/No Edits

Pull out your journal and allow your stream of consciousness to run freely. Write out all of your fears and any additional thoughts you have about this situation.

Then, try any of the four above-mentioned tools to shift away from catastrophic and/or all-or-nothing thinking.

For example, if you fear that your job interview is going to be an epic fail:

- Do a reality check. What is a more realistic outcome to your experience?
- On a scale of 1-10, how much of an impact will this interview have on your ENTIRE life?
- What could go *right*?
- What meditation from this book could you practice right now?

Chapter Seventeen

Resiliency and Stress Management

"The greatest glory in living lies not in never falling, but in rising every time we fall."
-Nelson Mandela

Meditation: Touchstones

Choose an item that you can easily keep in your pocket all day. This could be a crystal, a charm, or even a rock that you find on the side of the road. The object itself isn't important. The goal is to find something you can carry with you today.

Throughout the day, check in with this item. Notice how it feels. Notice how you feel checking in on it. Maybe you feel like this is a nuisance. Or maybe this activity feels like a nice time out from your day. Either way, check in with this item multiple times throughout the day.

At the end of the day, write about your experience of having to check in with this item.

If you enjoyed this activity, then what else could you "check in" with more regularly? For example, you can instead practice noticing your breath, or something you are grateful for? Use this activity as an opportunity to create more time for noticing things that support you and your core values.

Did you find this activity annoying? If so, this could be an opportunity for you to eliminate something you would like to STOP doing. For example, maybe you want to cut back on your screen time. Spend a day or two noticing how often you "check" your phone. Likely, you are in the habit of checking your phone far more than necessary. Can you replace that habit with something more supportive?

Use this touchstone activity to practice more mindfulness and let go of the things you are wasting time and energy on.

Resiliency

Given that life is fraught with curve balls, trials and tribulations, most of us (if not all of us) can attest to periods in our life where we struggled, didn't think we could make it through, endured such pain and yet we made it. Reflecting and remembering those times (because we forget) can help us to confirm and validate the **resilienc**y within us.

> Author Mark Manson: "You don't build resilience by feeling good all the time. You build resilience by getting better at feeling bad."[24]

In other words, resiliency gives you the emotional and mental strength to adapt, recover, and keep moving forward, even when the path appears unclear. Without resiliency, you might abandon your North Star journey at the first sign of difficulty. With resiliency, you learn from detours and use them to refine your direction.

Resilient people often reflect deeply after adversity. That reflection helps you understand what truly matters to you, clarify your values, recognize patterns in what gives you energy or drains you. This self-awareness is essential to identifying your North Star. The world is full of noise—expectations, comparisons, fear of missing out. Resiliency helps you stay grounded in your own journey, resisting the pull of paths that aren't meant for you.

Resiliency isn't just about bouncing back—**it's about bouncing forward**. Each challenge you overcome adds to your wisdom and confidence, helping you evolve into the person who can live out your North Star.

Once you glimpse your North Star, resiliency helps you stay committed. It's the inner resolve that says: "Even when it's hard, even when I doubt myself—I can keep going."

Stress Management

Finding your North Star involves making choices aligned with your values. Stress can lead to reactive or fear-based decisions. The path to purpose requires sustained effort. Stress drains your emotional and physical energy, making it harder to stay motivated. Effective stress management helps you recharge, stay focused and maintain momentum.

How we experience stress and how we are affected by it varies greatly. What is stressful for one, isn't for another, and our individual level of expression and coping can look very different. Not all stress is bad, in fact, some stress can motivate us, or push us to that next level. However, chronic stress can create a tremendous strain on our minds and bodies. The big three ways that stress can manifest and signal/warn us are physically, behaviorally, and emotionally.

In fact, a growing body of research shows that stress contributes to a wide range of health issues including:

- High blood pressure
- Heart disease, including heart rhythm disorders and coronary artery disease
- Digestive conditions, including irritable bowel syndrome, acid reflux and peptic ulcers
- Lack of sleep
- Obesity
- Headaches
- Backaches
- Anxicty
- Depression

Stress pulls you outward—towards tasks, expectations, and distractions. Managing it allows you to turn inward, where your North Star lives. Practices like mindfulness, journaling, or quiet reflection help you tune into your intuition, recognize patterns in your passions, and feel more connected to your authentic self.

Activity 1: Finding Your Resilience

Think back to a time when you were faced with difficulty. Ask yourself the following and write in your journal:

- What was it that enabled you to get through? What strategies did you use? (These should go in your working well if they relate to your current goal.)

- What understanding/beliefs did you hold on to, and what solutions/actions did you find?

Activity 2: Noticing Your Stress

Ask yourself the following and write in your journal:

- How do you know when you are stressed?
- What does stress look like/sound like/feel like when it shows up?
- What do you notice?
- Where do you feel the stress in your body?
- What do those around you notice?

Activity 3: Creating Your Emotional Safety Plan

- Create your emotional safety plan using the blank ESPG form.
- In each quad, put the answers to the questions in the grid.
- Carry this in your wallet, take a picture of it with your phone, keep it readily available so you can activate your plan at any time in case of an emotional emergency!

Emotional Safety Plan

An emotional safety plan can assist you when you are experiencing stress and/or other strong emotional reactions. By creating your plan ahead of time, you will be prepared for what you can do in that moment to help regulate, ground, and attend to your feelings/reactions.[25]

1. What immediate actions can you take in the moment when feeling stressed and overwhelmed?	3. Identify a safety network person and what actions you want/need them to take to help support you with your actions/plan.
2. How will you know those actions are helping you?	4 How will your network person know if your plan is working?

Brigitta's Emotional Safety Plan

1. What immediate actions can you take in the moment when feeling stressed and overwhelmed? *Take a moment to simply breathe. If possible, step away from the situation. Ask myself, "Is there anything I can do, in this moment, to support resolution in this situation?*	3. Identify a safety network person and what actions you want/need them to take to help support you with your actions/plan. *I can check in with my accountability groups, video chat with close friends on Marco Polo or check in with a sober sister.*
2. How will you know those actions are helping you? *I can think clear thoughts. I might even be able to brainstorm a little bit. If this is not a chronic situation, I might do something like take a walk*	4 How will your network person know if your plan is working? *They know I am feeling better when I crack a joke or find humor in the situation.*

Peggi's Emotional Safety Plan.

1. What immediate actions can you take in the moment when feeling stressed and overwhelmed? *I take deep breaths or do my right hand on heart, left hand in chin exercise, write in my journal, take a walk.*	3. Identify a safety network person and what actions you want/need them to take to help support you with your actions/plan. *I have several friends I can call, use WhatsApp, and text strings I can utilize.*
3. How will you know those actions are helping you? *I can actually feel my central nervous system calming down, and I can think more clearly.*	4 How will your network person know if your plan is working? *I usually end the conversations by thanking them.*

Gnora reminds us: Flexibility is NOT to be underestimated. Changing things up can sometimes lead to wonderful breakthroughs.

Chapter Eighteen

Take a Walk

"When we walk, the two halves of our brains converse. Walking is an excellent way to form ideas. Walking, especially alone, clears the mind and gives the mind space to roam."
—Julia Cameron

Meditation: This chapter is a form of meditation in and of itself.

Both of us can attest to the magic of the practice of walking. Julia Cameron is also a fan: "The goal is to connect to a world outside of us, to lose the obsessive self-focus of self-exploration and simply, explore. One quickly notes that when the mind is focused on other things, the self often comes into a far more accurate focus."[26]

Walking has a quiet power that goes far beyond physical movement—it's deeply connected to clarity, intention, and alignment with our inner compass, our North Star path.

Walking in silence (that means no podcasts, audio books, Spotify, or gab sessions with besties) can be magical. When we walk, especially without distractions, our minds begin to settle. The rhythm of our steps often mirrors the rhythm of our thoughts, allowing insight to surface naturally. This reflective state helps us reconnect with our deeper values and intentions.

Walking brings us into our bodies and into the moment. When we're grounded, we're less likely to be swept away by external pressures or internal noise. That presence helps us hear the quiet voice of our intuition—the one that points toward our North Star.

Each step is a metaphor for progress. Even when we feel stuck, walking reminds us that movement is possible. It's a physical affirmation that we're capable of moving forward, one step at a time, toward what matters the most.

A weekly walk in solitude can become a time out for self-care. This practice can become a sanctuary that you look forward to every week. Plus, it's free! Stepping away from your day to simply walk and listen can completely transform the way you approach your days.

Ultimately, walking without distraction is a moving mediation where you become the receptor for internal guidance from your intuition. It helps you tune in to your quieter, more creative thoughts. It's a tool for refueling your imagination and refreshing your brain.

Activity 1: Go For a Walk

Trust us, you won't do this unless you schedule it, so go do that now! Choose a day and time to walk for a minimum of 15 minutes.

Then, when you walk, notice what you see, hear, smell, and feel. Notice your thoughts. Are you worrying? Are you reviewing things? Are you brooding? Are you planning ahead? Are you remembering things? Are you talking to yourself? Anything worth noting?

Just notice.

Notice what ideas "pop" into your head. Notice who you think about. Notice how you're feeling.

If you feel inclined to talk with your intuition, walking is a great time to ask it for assistance. Ask open-ended questions and see where your mind goes in response. (If information flows, pull out your smartphone and voice record these thoughts to revisit later.)

Allow for any "thought tangents" that may occur as well as moments where it seems that there are no thoughts at all.

When you get home, journal about your experience. Include any of your thoughts, ideas, surprises, as well as any brainstorming or solutions you may have thought of.

And schedule your next walk!

This reflective tool may become your favorite stress-busting tactic. After several strolls, notice how much clearer your journey towards your North Star becomes.

Brigitta's example:

I've been utilizing this tool for so long; I have come to rely on it as my "go to" problem-solving technique. Back in 2010, I co-wrote the short film, "Stalkers" with my friend, Dawn. Dawn and I spent hours creating the best script we could. Our goal was to create an outstanding film (we were also to be the co-stars) that would win awards at festivals and generate more work for us as actresses, all of which happened! "Stalkers" was included in 20 indie film festivals and won many awards in the process.

Making a film takes TONS of work. And if the script isn't great, the film is destined to fail.

Dawn and I worked well together and had a clear vision of the characters, the plot, etc. Neither of us found the writing to be difficult, except for one big problem; we hit a massive "writers block" when it came to the ending. For short films, having a great ending is crucial if you want to be remembered. We spent hours in front of the computer only to come away without a memorable ending. One day, after having spent another afternoon getting nowhere, we looked at each other and threw up our hands in total surrender. We admitted the obvious—we were stuck. We were utterly stumped as to how to end this film. In frustration, we went for a walk. We were too tired and disheartened even to talk to one another. We just walked in silence.

And then, an idea popped into my head...not just an idea...THE idea for our perfect ending. This was a plot twist that nobody would ever see coming.

As a filmmaker, sitting in the audience and listening to their responses is indescribable. It's nothing short of amazing to hear their laughter and audible gasps when they are fully engaged in your film. Hearing the audience's reaction to our ending was a highlight I'll never forget. We believe this ending was the main reason we went on to win the "audience choice" award repeatedly. Our ending was shocking, hilarious, and totally in alignment with our story and vision.

I can promise you, we would never have come up with that plot twist had we remained seated in front of that computer. Our silent walk handed us our magic wand.

Peggi's example:

I often walk in silence when I need ideas for my social media posts, my weekly newsletter, and contributions to magazines and topics for meetings I facilitate. I use the Notes app on my iPhone to record any thoughts that come up. It is truly amazing that I often start my walk with the writer's block Brigitta talked about and end with ideas I can use for my various writing projects and facilitation topic ideas.

Gnora comments: The best ideas can't find you when you're sitting still, staring at screens! Sometimes the most productive thing you can do is take your brain for a walk and let it wander.

Chapter Nineteen

Asking for Help

"Lean on me. When you're not strong. And I'll be your friend. I'll help you carry on."
-Bill Withers

Meditation

Using Disruption to be Present
If you live or work where there is unavoidable noise (i.e. airplanes flying overhead) use this consistent "interruption" to be present.

The best way to describe this is to use a personal example.

Brigitta's examples of using disruption to be present:

I used to live next to the Vancouver General Hospital Emergency building. The sound of sirens was constant. That was when I discovered the value of this exercise. Every time I heard the emergency vehicles, I'd stop what I was doing and take a deep breath. (I also would send a silent prayer for the person in need of immediate help!). This meant I was stopping and becoming present multiple times a day.

More recently, I attended a class on flower arranging. Although the teacher's studio was gorgeous, it was also on the flight path of an international airport. This meant that every ten minutes, a plane would soar over her workshop space. She utilized this perfectly. Every time we heard a plane, we took a step back from our arrangement to get a different perspective on our design. This is an important but often overlooked component for creating a lovely arrangement. Those jumbo jets were a perfect reminder for us to stop, step back, and be present with our work.

Experiment with how you can use your environmental "disruptions" as an opportunity to become present.

Asking for Help is NOT a sign of weakness; it's actually a strength.

Here is the truth…You will never be "great" at something you have to work really hard just to be good at. Focusing too much energy on things other than your strengths will not only waste a lot of time but leave you feeling frustrated as well. But, if you put that time and energy into your natural talents, you will likely succeed with more efficiency (and enjoyment.)

What can you delegate to someone else? Is there someone you could hire to take over this area of your goal? Can you barter a trade of some sort so you can offer your strengths to their goals, while they do the same for you?

Utilize and cultivate your strengths. (Hint: your strengths are usually the things you feel confident doing.) And whenever possible, delegate your tasks that require your weaker skills to someone who's better at it than you.

Having said that, some of our weaknesses do indeed need to be addressed before we can more effectively move forward in our lives. In order to achieve our goals, we may need to learn some skills and eliminate some bad habits. To successfully navigate those challenges, we may require help.

This is why therapists, coaches, trainers, etc. exist. People naturally want to help others. There is always someone out there who you can go to for help.

And for those of you who think asking for help is a sign of weakness, we won't candy-coat it; **you're wrong.** Ask any successful business owner if they did it all themselves, and we assure you, they will say they had to get a lot of help along the way. If you're stuck …ask for help!

Peggi's example:

I tried to address my problematic drinking by myself, and I was intermittently successful. I would stop drinking for months, and the year my daughter got married, I managed almost a year. But I always found an excuse to go back. I justified because I could stop when I wanted; I could moderate. In the end, I almost lost my marriage and my family. The day I put my wineglass down for good, Jenn Kautsch's Sober Sis 21 Day Reset program flashed across my Facebook page. I immediately signed up. There, I found the kind of support and community I needed.

Since that time, I have enrolled in many other alcohol-free programs and now I am giving back by facilitating my own. At the time of publishing this book, I will have been alcohol-free for almost seven years.

Brigitta's Example:

Joining a Support Group to overcome Bulimia:

Living with disordered eating presents its own challenges because you have to eat every day. This is not like quitting smoking. You can survive without cigarettes (although I felt like I couldn't when I first quit!) You cannot survive without food. It's because of this that I've labeled this particular issue as the "gift that keeps on giving". It has the potential to be an opportunity for growth every single day with every meal and snack you consume.

Having said that, it can also be a terrifying proposition to be faced with your inner demons every time you eat. (Or every time you choose to NOT eat).

"The opposite of addiction is connection" -Johann Hari

Although disordered eating may not be considered an addiction, the isolation and shame it breeds is the same. The very act of reaching out for help can feel monumental when we are in the throes of our turmoil around food. And this very action, reaching out for support, can be the one thing that helps us out of these treacherous waters.

I was in my early thirties when I discovered Geneen Roth (Emotional Eating Guru for many). When she offered her online "Women, Food, and God" community, I jumped at the opportunity. Zoom didn't exist back then. This was perfect for me. I didn't have to show my face. I could listen and participate anonymously because the shame I felt was deadening.

I will never forget that first group call. Geneen talked us through a visualization, spoke to us about the topic for that evening, and then opened up the call to all of us. Hearing the voices of other women with EXACTLY the same struggles as me was undeniably life-changing. That was my baby step to healing my shattered self-esteem. I knew from that moment forward; I was not alone and that help was literally a phone call away.

Activity 1: Asking for Help Inventory (Journal)

- Where are you stuck?
- Is this something you can delegate?
- Can you ask someone for help?
- Do you need to hire someone to support you or learn new skills?
- Decide which of these action items will be most helpful to you and go get the help you need.

Another "asking for help" example from Brigitta: Joining an Accountability Group

I never thought I needed an "accountability group". After all, I'm a life coach. I am absolutely a self-starter, and procrastination is just not an issue for me. If I say I'm going to do something, I do it…simple. Why join an accountability group? For the help. I can honestly say my business has grown more in the two years of being involved with this group than in the entire previous decade. Why? Asking for help is an integral part of our itinerary at every meeting. There is zero shame in asking for support. We actively look for ways to help each other.

And because we are all talented and accomplished in very different ways, someone always has a great solution to any problem offered.

Fun fact: we have become an example of what a successful accountability group looks like in our community.

Another "asking for help" example from Peggi:

I knew that when I wrote my first book, This Side of Alcohol, that I would need to create a social media presence. I can write well, but I know that my knowledge of social media was sadly lacking. I knew that one of my UC Davis colleagues, Kaitlyn Ash, was also a business coach. One year before my book was published, she set up my website, Facebook Page, Instagram, LinkedIn, created a TSOA brand and logo, newsletter, and set up a content schedule for my writing. Four and a half years later, my community tops 25 thousand followers, and I just get to do what I love, and that is to write.

Chapter Twenty

What's Next? Clearing the Slate

"Obstacles are put in your way to see if what you want is really worth fighting for."
--Zig Ziglar

Meditation: Flooding with Gratitude

Stand tall and close your eyes. Feel your feet planted firmly on the ground. Take several deep breaths, following your inhales and exhales.

Remember an experience when you were filled with gratitude. Really feel it as if it were happening again right now.

Next. Remember another experience. Feel this one fully.
Then remember another experience.

Next, remember a time you laughed so hard you cried. Feel it fully.
Remember another time, and another…

FLOOD yourself with memories of gratitude and laughter for one minute.

(If you do this daily, you will start to discover more memories/achievements.)

Clearing the Slate

When we carry emotional baggage, regrets, or outdated beliefs, it's like trying to navigate with a fogged-up compass. Clearing the slate allows you to let go of what no longer serves you, making space for clarity and alignment with your true direction.

Your North Star requires presence, intention, and awareness. If your mind is cluttered with unresolved issues, distractions, or limiting narratives, it's harder to hear your inner guidance. A clear slate is like a quiet room—you can finally hear your own voice.

What can you clear off your desk? Where are you wasting time and leaking energy that you could utilize towards achieving your goals? Yes, we all have 24 hours in the day, but they are not the same hours for each of us. Some of us have children at home, some of us work 60 hours a week, some of us are caring for older parents, and some of us are starting an entirely new chapter of our lives. Our time is a precious resource, and how we use it matters.

Our energy is a finite resource. Burning the candle at both ends always leads to overwhelm and exhaustion. Budgeting both of these resources is key to enjoying our journey.

If you think of your time and energy as currency, hard-earned cash, what would you invest in?

Letting go of old stories helps you reclaim your agency. It's a way of saying, "I am not defined by my past—I choose my path forward." That mindset is essential for staying aligned with your purpose, especially when the journey gets tough.

Finally, a clean slate is fertile ground. It invites new ideas, relationships, and opportunities that are in harmony with your North Star. When you're not weighed down, you're more open to inspiration and serendipity.

Gnora adds: Clearing your slate isn't about erasing your story — it's about making room for the next beautiful chapter! Sometimes you need to declutter your heart the same way you declutter your closet.

Activity 1: Reflective Journaling

"Let Go, or Be Dragged." -Zen Proverb

Write freely about:

- What you're holding onto emotionally or mentally.
- What beliefs or habits no longer serve you.
- What you're ready to release.

Prompt ideas:

- What am I ready to let go of?
- What story have I been telling myself that needs rewriting?
- What does a clean slate look like for me?
- Could you try something different or new and still fulfill the desire that the original goal was meant to achieve?

Sit with this awhile. These are not easy questions to ask. Inquire with as much honesty and self-compassion as you can. These questions are worth asking and answering.

You may, after thinking about it, decide to let it go. By doing so, you've just released some stuck energy that you can redirect to a more aligned goal. (Remember to be compassionate with yourself.)

Or, you may decide, "Absolutely NO! I'm not letting it go." And in that realization, you will discover more clarity as to why you must keep this as a North Star goal.

Activity 2: Letting Go Ritual

Create a symbolic act of release:

- Write down what you want to release on paper, then burn it (safely).
- Tear it up and bury it.
- Release it into water (like a river or ocean) using biodegradable paper.

This physical act helps your mind and body register the shift.

Activity 3: Letter to Self

Below are some prompts, but you are not bound by them. Your writing will take you where you need to go.

Dear ______________________________,

I cannot believe how much I experienced this year.

I decided to ____

I let go of ____

I welcomed ____

I said goodbye to ____

I surprised myself with ____

I dreamed ____

I created ____

I learned ____

I pulled some things off I didn't think I could do! I ______________________________

I am most grateful for ____

I am so proud of ____

My wish for myself going forward is ______________________________

Peggi Cooney and Brigitta Dau

Chapter Twenty one

Social Media: Friend or Foe?

"Almost everything will work again if you unplug it for a few minutes, including you."
- Anne Lamott

Meditation: Gratitude Expansion

Either sitting or standing, close your eyes and take in a few deep breaths.

Bring to mind a moment from your past when you felt true gratitude.
What was happening?
Who was with you?
Picture your gratitude glowing in your heart and radiating outward- so vividly that the people involved can feel it. Even if they are no longer in your life, imagine them receiving your gratitude. Notice how it feels to offer it to them.

Now, recall another experience of gratitude and repeat this practice.

Take a moment to notice how you feel as your gratitude expands.

So how can we liberate ourselves from this excessive time-suck?

Finding your North Star is a deeply personal journey. Social media can be a tool or a trap—it depends on whether you're using it to amplify your voice or drown it out. Social media can both support and sabotage your life's purpose—depending on how you use it. It offers connection and inspiration, but also distraction, comparison, identity confusion, and isolation.

According to DataReportal's 2025 Global Digital Report, the average person spends 2 hours and 21 minutes per day on social media platforms. That's almost 17 hours a week, 68 hours a month, and over 800 hours a year! Not only can social media be a black hole of time, but it can also take a toll on our mental health. Recent research shows that spending more time on social media is linked to greater symptoms of depression.[27]

From the Mass Planner Social Media News:

> The advent of social media in contemporary society is undoubtedly one of the most revolutionary phenomena of our time. While the impact of social media can be beneficial, it can also have negative implications on our psychological, emotional, and social well-being. Consequently, it is critical to recognize the intricate web of interactions that social media has on our lives and develop strategies to harness its benefits positively.
>
> Social media offers a multitude of advantages, including enabling us to connect with people from diverse cultures and backgrounds worldwide. Furthermore, social media platforms offer a plethora of knowledge and information, promoting personal growth and development. The platform also creates avenues for individuals to exhibit their skills and talents to a broader audience, potentially launching them into the limelight. The ability of social media to encourage self-expression and creativity cannot be overemphasized.[28]

Here's a deeper look at how it influences your journey toward meaning:

Positive Impacts of Social Media on Finding Your North Star:

- Connection to Communities: Social media can help you discover like-minded groups, movements, or mentors that align with your values and passions.
- Exposure to Ideas: Platforms like YouTube, Instagram, and LinkedIn expose you to diverse lifestyles, careers, and philosophies, potentially sparking new interests or goals.
- Support and Encouragement: Online networks can offer emotional support, validation, and encouragement, especially when you're exploring unconventional paths.

The Mass Planner Social Media News agrees that social media can be a source of inspiration and motivation:

> Social media can be an enigmatic and bewildering source of inspiration and motivation, evoking complex feelings and thoughts in individuals. By selectively following people and accounts that align with their deeply ingrained personal and professional goals, individuals can be propelled into a realm of inspiration and motivation that may help them to achieve their aspirations. Social media can also provide unprecedented access to resources and information that can be instrumental in catalyzing personal and professional growth.[29]

Negative Impacts That Can Derail Your North Star Trek:

- Constant Comparison: Seeing curated success stories and highlight reels can make you question your own path, leading to feelings of inadequacy or confusion.
- Distraction and Overstimulation: The endless scroll pulls you away from introspection and real-world experiences that are essential for discovering purpose.
- Identity Fragmentation: Trying to fit into online personas or trends can dilute your authentic self, making it harder to identify what truly matters to you.
- Mental Health Strain: Excessive use is linked to anxiety, depression, and FOMO (fear of missing out), which can cloud judgment and reduce motivation.

The Mass Planner Social Media News also warns:

The effects of social media can be unfavorable, impacting personal growth and development negatively. Individuals are vulnerable to addiction, social comparison, feelings of inadequacy, and negative self-image. Additionally, social media can erode focus and distract us from real-life social interactions.[30]

How to Use Social Media Purposefully

- Curate Your Feed: Follow accounts that inspire growth, creativity, and authenticity.
- Set Boundaries: Limit time spent online to protect your mental clarity and focus.
- Reflect Offline: Use journaling, nature, or conversations to reconnect with your inner compass.
- Don't Trust, Verify: It's so easy to use Chat GPT or Copilot to get information. They are not always accurate. These platforms can be helpful, but make sure you do your research by using other sources.
- Share Intentionally: Post content that reflects your values and aspirations—not just what gets likes.

As Gnora's puts it: Wasting precious time scrolling or living vicariously through someone else' Facebook feed sounds like a total drag. I'd rather be out living my own adventure!

Activity 1: Detox your feed.

Open your favorite platform - Facebook, Instagram, or TikTok, and look through the accounts you follow. If you don't know or genuinely care about them, unfollow them. Your feed should be filled with accounts that inspire you, uplift you, support your growth, or simply make you smile. Yes, this might even mean unfollowing some friends. If someone's posts make you feel bad about yourself, it's okay to step back.

(Side Note: Glenn Macintosh, Australia's leading "Food Psych" does this as a first step with his teen clients struggling with disordered eating. Parents are often surprised until they realize their teens spend more time scrolling than talking to anyone else, including them. Their social feeds have more influence than any real-life connection.)

Activity 2: Switch your Phone's Settings to Black and White.

Social media is designed to entrap us with bright colors and constant stimulation. By switching your phone's screen to black and white, you strip away much of its lure. A quick Google search will show you how to adjust your phone's settings.

Notice how much easier it is to disengage when your screen is only various shades of grey.

Activity 3: Turn off notifications.

Every ping, buzz, and flash is a subtle invitation to distraction.

Turning off notifications is one of the simplest and most powerful ways to reclaim your time - and peace.

Activity 4: Keep your phone OFF for one full day.

Brigitta's personal example of a "PHONE OFF" day.

I remember the first time I tried this. I had seriously underestimated how attached I was to my phone. I was shocked - and honestly a little horrified - by how often I instinctively reached for it. Even worse was noticing how uneasy I felt without the constant distraction. But then something wonderful happened. I suddenly had so much "free time" I could feel myself exhale. Now, I take a "PHONE OFF day every two weeks. It feels downright luxurious.

Gnorth suggests that turning off your phone, even briefly, gives you space to focus on what really matters...like working on your North Star goals.

Wrapping it up

"Don't die with your music still in you."
-Wayne Dyer

Our hope is that this workbook offered you a practical, structured, reflective, and empowering way for you to discover and stay aligned with your life's purpose, your North Star. The exercises, prompts and tools are transferable in both your personal and professional areas of growth. We hope you gained clarity and direction.

As we close this book, remember this is not the end. It's the beginning.

You've explored the terrain of your inner world, navigated the storm of doubt, and charted a course toward your North Star. Along the way, you have honed in on your purpose, passion, and possibility. You've asked hard questions, embraced your truth, and dared to imagine a life aligned with who you truly are. You have gained confidence on your path and a stronger commitment to follow your heart.

But the journey doesn't stop here.

Remember that your North Star is not a destination; it's a direction. It's the compass that guides you through the unknown, the whisper that reminds you of your worth, and the fire that fuels your courage when the path gets steep.

There will be days when the way forward gets cloudy. On those days, use this workbook as a long-lasting personal resource you can revisit to stay grounded, especially during times of change, doubt, or transition. Look inward, trust the wisdom you've discovered. Trust the wisdom you've cultivated. Trust the strength you've discovered. Trust that even when you feel lost, your North Star is still shining, waiting for you to look up and believe.

You are not alone. Every step you take toward your truth sends a ripple into the world, inspiring others to seek their own light. Our wish is that you share your unique gifts generously with the world. Your journey matters. Your voice matters. You matter.

So go forward with boldness. Let your heart lead. Let your purpose shine.

Keep in touch; all our contact info is at the end of this book. We would absolutely LOVE to hear from you.

Gnorth and Gnora want to remind you: "You are braver than you believe, stronger than you seem, and smarter than you think." -A.A. Milne

Final and Very Important Thoughts...

When You Need a Little Extra Help

How can we differentiate between self-help and the need for therapy?

We wrote this book to support you with your personal growth. All of the tools we have provided are powerful, but therapy adds structure, containment, and specialized care.

Seeking therapy is in no way a sign of failure. We both agree that utilizing therapy is in and of itself a form of self-care.

Gnorth is adamant about this. Needing the support of a therapist does not mean you are weak. It means you are wise enough to know that healing matters.

How do you know if you should investigate working with a therapist?

- You feel stuck in repeating patterns
- Anxiety, depression, or trauma symptoms persist
- Relationships or work are suffering
- You can't access joy, creativity, or peace for long stretches
- Your self-care tools aren't helping as they used to

If you wish to seek support:

- Talk to your doctor, or look for therapists aligned with your values (mind-body, trauma-informed, spiritually open)
- Trust your intuition—find someone you feel safe and seen with
- Try one session; you're not committing forever

Therapy can coexist beautifully with other modalities such as coaching, energy healing, or art therapy—each supports a different layer. If you feel like you are carrying everything alone and something inside still feels tangled, it's time to reach out. Again, see this as an act of deep self-respect. Seeking professional help isn't giving up; it's widening your circle of care.

Acknowledgements

"We cannot do this thing alone." –Laura McKowen

Thank you.

To our beta readers: Stacy, Christina, Dawn, Lauren, Whitney, Laura, and Tony, who were not afraid to give us honest feedback.

To our amazing editor: Val Hudson at Valanne. We love that you love Gnorth and Gnora.

To our brilliant cover designer: Stacy Morin. We hope this convinces you that you are an artist.

To Robin Nelson and Leaning Rock Press: Thank you for all your patience.

To Lisa Roeber Photography: Who happens to be Peggi's lovely daughter-in-law and mother to Ryan.

And to all the people who have touched our lives in some way. We love you to the North Star and back.

Recommended Reading/Resources

James Clear: *Atomic Habits*
Insight Timer App
Becky Vollmer: *You Are Not Stuck*
Denzel Washington: Fall Forward Speech Commencement
Richard Schwartz: *No Bad Parts*
Geneen Roth: *Women, Food, and God*
Johann Hari: TED talk: "The Opposite of Addiction is Not Sobriety - It's Connection
David D.Burns: *Feeling Good, the new mood therapy*
Julia Cameron: *The Artist's Way*
Byron Katie: *Loving What Is*
MastinKipp: *Daily Love*
Danielle LaPort: *The Desire Map*
Bessel Van Der Kolk, M.D.: *The Body Keeps the Score*
Sark: *Succulent Wild Woman*
Austin Kleon: *Steal Like an Artist*
Dr. Ingrid Clayton: *Fawning*
Mark Manson: *The Subtle Art of Giving an F*ck*
Suleika Jaouad: *The Book of Alchemy*

Contributors

Peggi Cooney:

peggicooney@gmail.com
thissideofalcohol@gmail.com
#peggicooney
#thissideofalcohol
Facebook.com/groups/thissideofalcohol
thissideofalcohol.com
zeroproofexperiences.com

Brigitta Dau:
brigittadau@brigittadau.com
brigittadau.com
Facebook.com/Brigitta Dau Coaching
instagram.com/BrigittaDauCoaching
Instagram.com/Brigitta.YarnPigCrafts

Peggi Cooney is a social worker, author, speaker, facilitator, and alcohol freedom advocate. She holds a MSW and has 26 years of experience in Child Welfare and Adult Protective Services. She is currently a social work instructor/coach for UC Davis: Professional and Continuing Education. She published her first book, This Side of Alcohol: Random Thoughts and Candid Words of Pain, Hope, Humor and Love – and All that is Possible in Sobriety in 2021. She is the Chief Connections Officer for award-winning Zero Proof Experiences/Sober in the City/ZPE Connect where she partners with founder Susie Streelman to host alcohol-free events all over the world and facilitate weekly membership meetings. In 2024, Peggi received the Dry Society Social Club's 2024 National People's Choice Award for her work in the world of recovery. She lives with her husband, Paul, in West Sacramento and Lake Almanor, California. Together they have five adult children and thirteen grandchildren.

Brigitta Dau is a certified Life Coach, Pilates instructor, Reiki master, crafting teacher, author of Crafting a Better Life – Creative Approaches to Personal Growth, and Etsy shop owner. Guiding people towards their best selves has always been her passion. Brigitta was a professional actress throughout the late 80s and 90s, where she worked in TV and film in both Canada and the USA. This unique experience combined with her interest in empowerment and creative expression helped shape her work as a life coach, speaker, and teacher. Throughout all of life's detours, she's always had the loving support of her husband, Doug. They live in Los Angeles, California, and enjoy the humorous and often hardheaded companionship of their naughty pooch, Stanley.

Endnotes

1. Oliver, Mary. "The Summer Day." Retrieved January 3, 2025 from https://www.loc.gov/programs/poetry-and-literature/poet-laureate/poet-laureate-projects/poetry-180/all-poems/item/poetry-180-133/the-summer-day/
2. Cameron Julia, The Artist's Way, Penguin Random House LLC, NY, NY, 1992.
3. Carter, Rita Mapping of the Mind, University of California Press, Oakland, CA, 2010.
4. Tahsin Arzu, Davidson Rosemary, Craftfulnes, Quercus Edition Ltd, Great Britain, 2018.

5 Chaplin, Angie. The Way Onward: A Companion Guide to The Leadership Challenge Self Empowered for Behavioral Health Professionals. Licensed facilitator curriculum, 2025. https://www.thewayonward.com.

6. Gilbert, Elizabeth. "Not This" Essay. Retrieved October 10, 2025 from https://splitfyi.com/wp-content/uploads/2023/02/Downloadable-Not-This-by-Elizabeth-Gilbert.pdf.
7. Bell, Rob. The Robcast. Episode #303: South Star. Friday, March 12, 2021.
8. Vollmer, Becky. You Are Not Stuck. St. Martin's Publishing Group. New York, NY. 2023.
9. Boxall, Michelle. The Curious Coach: "Finding Your North Star." Retrieved March 30, 2025 from https://thecuriouscoach.org/finding-your-north-star/
10. Kipp, Mastin, Claim Your Power, Hay House Inc. Carlsbad, CA, 2020.
11. Laporte, Danielle, The Desire Map, Sounds True. Louisville, CO, 2014.
12. Appel, Elliot. Write Your Own Obituary. Retrieved January 12, 2025 from https://kindnessfp.com/write-your-own-obituary/
13. Bollinger, Austin. Crash Your Goals! The Ultimate Guide to Achieving Consistent Success. 2021. B&b, LLC. Nashville, Tennesee.
14. Oettingens, Gabrielle. "Rethinking Positive Thinking: How Gabrielle Oettingen's WOOP Method Transforms Goal-Setting." Retrieved January 12, 2025 from https://www.linkedin.com/pulse/rethinking-positive-thinking-how-gabrielle-oettingens-medet-ali-qewueWOOP
15. Clear, James. Atomic Habits. 2018. Avery/Peguin Random House. New York, New York.
16. Casey Family Programs. The Coaching Toolkit for Child Welfare Practice. University of California, Davis. Revised June 2013.
17. Tracy, Brian. The 80-20 Rule—The Pareto Principle." Retrieved November 14, 2025 from https://www.briantracy.com/blog/personal-success/how-to-use-the-80-20-rule-pareto-principle/?srsltid=AfmBOor-sYTtp7UjsQ2x-HrxY2GJ0M4zqqiBTIv4euSm6PJuxe3RT-hV

18 The Imposter Syndrome, retrieved August 24, 2025 from https://impostersyndrome.com.au/index.php/questionnaires/

19. Beck, Aaron T. Cognitive Behavioral Therapy and Emotional Disorders. International Universities Press. New York. 1974.
20. Cameron Julia, The Artist's Way, Penguin Random House LLC, NY, NY, 1992.
21. Davidson B. From Dark to Light: A Modern Mystic's Guide to Healing and Spiritual Awakening. Hay House Australia. October 2019.

22. Lohrbach, Sue. "The Consultation and Information Sharing Framework." Retrieved January 12, 2025 from https://humanservices.ucdavis.edu/toolkits/safety-organized-practice/about-sop
23. Schwartz, R., Sweezy, M. and Schwartz, R. Internal Family Systems: Trauma-Informed Treatment for Anxiety, Depression, PTSD & Substance Abuse. PESI Publishing, Inc. WI. 2017.
24. Manson, Mark. "Your Next Breakthrough: The Secret to Resilience" weekly email. October 6, 2025.
25. University of California Davis: Continuing and Professional Education. "Using SOP for Resiliency Building in CW Staff". Davis, CA. January 2024.
26. Cameron Julia, The Artist's Way, Penguin Random House LLC, NY, NY, 1992.
27. DataReportal, Digital 2025: Global Overview Report (We Are Social & Meltwater, 2025)
28. Mass Planner Social Media News. "Exploring How Social Media Impacts Personal Development and Growth." Retrieved November 12, 2025 from https://www.massplanner.com/exploring-how-social-media-impacts-personal-development-and-growth/#:~:text=Social%20media%20can%20be%20a%20source%20of%20inspiration%20and%20motivation,catalyzing%20personal%20and%20professional%20growth
29. Ibid. Mass Planner Social Media News.
30. Ibid. Mass Planner Social Media News.

www.ingramcontent.com/pod-product-compliance
Ingram Content Group UK Ltd.
Pitfield, Milton Keynes, MK11 3LW, UK
UKHW061959290726
14090UKWH00021B/1298

9 781960 596833